Sacred Records

Sacred Records

Perspectives

On The

Records

That Have Shaped

Sports

History

Edited by Greg Echlin

ADDAX
PUBLISHING
GROUP

Published by Addax Publishing Group, Inc.
Copyright © 1999 by Greg Echlin
Designed by Laura Bolter
Cover Designed by Laura Bolter

For Information address:
Addax Publishing Group, Inc.
8643 Hauser Drive, Suite 235, Lenexa, KS 66215

ISBN: 1-886110-74-3

Distributed to the trade by Andrews McMeel Publishing
4520 Main Street
Kansas City, MO 64111

Printed in the USA

1 3 5 7 9 10 8 6 4 2

ATTENTION: SCHOOLS AND BUSINESSES
Addax Publishing Group, Inc. books are available at quantity discounts with bulk purchase for education, business, or sales promotional use. For information, please write to: Special Sales Department, Addax Publishing Group
8643 Hauser Drive, Suite 235, Lenexa, Kansas 66215

Library of Congress Cataloging-in-Publication Data

Sacred records : perspectives on the records that have shaped sports

history / edited by Greg Echlin.

    p. cm.

    ISBN 1-886110-74-3 (alk. paper)

    1. Sports records—United States. 2. Sports—United States-

-History. I. Echlin, Greg, 1956- .

GV741.S32 199

796'.0973—dc21   99-14866
                                                            CIP

Dedication

To the late Frank J. Echlin

Table of Contents

Chapter 12:
5,714, Nolan Ryan's All-Time Strikeout Record
The Fan's View:

The Veteran's View:

Acknowledgments

First and foremost, I could undertake no project without the support of my family. My wife Ticia and our children Ian and Emily have been great, especially the patience they displayed through my hectic stretches. I love all of you.

Through my work in the sports journalism industry, I've encountered many wonderful people in and outside the arena. It was with pleasure I worked with all the contributors for their perspectives covered in these pages. Some I knew from previous interviews, some I knew of from working in their midst and some I've met for the first time through mutual acquaintances.

My thanks to Bob Snodgrass for giving me the opportunity to work with him, to Darcie Kidson for her patience while I bounce around from office to office and to Michelle Washington for helping me prepare for the millennium with improved computer skills.

I would also like to thank KMBZ Radio for allowing me the flexibility between balancing my work there and running Greg Echlin Sports Services. As has often been the case, much of the work conveniently blends together.

Introduction

I t is interesting to observe how throughout the 20th century certain athletes are associated with specific numbers and not just the ones worn on their jerseys. Before Hank Aaron broke Babe Ruth's all-time home run record, even the casual sports fan knew that Ruth formerly held the record at 714. Today, how many of the same casual fans do you think could instantly rattle off Aaron's all-time home run total (755)? As quickly as 714? It's a matter of opinion.

Until Mark McGwire and Sammy Sosa broke Roger Maris' single-season home run record, do you know anyone who didn't know that Maris hit 61 in 1961? Or that Maris surpassed Ruth's previous total of 60? The number 70 has its place in history now and might end up being as identified with McGwire as much as 714 is identified with Ruth.

Joe DiMaggio's record of hitting in 56 straight games in 1941 has withstood the test of time. If you cover up DiMaggio's name, but associate the number 56 with baseball, chances are you'll think of the DiMaggio record. Before Cal Ripken stamped the number 2,632 into the record books, most still remember that Lou Gehrig played in 2,130 straight games. And this is one of the more memorable of the great numbers Gehrig posted in his Hall of Fame career. He still holds the American League record for RBIs in one

season with 184 in 1931. As *Baltimore Sun* writer Ken
Rosenthal spells out in his perspective on Cal Ripken's
streak, the Orioles infielder has racked up some other
outstanding numbers during his career, but his name
will be forever associated with The Streak.

If you think college basketball and say, "88," how
quick are you to think of the UCLA winning streak? If
you think NBA basketball and say, "33," how quick are
you to remember the Los Angeles Lakers' 33 straight
wins in 1972? As you will find out, *Chicago Tribune*
writer Sam Smith feels the number 72 for the Chicago
Bulls' victory total in 1996 carries greater weight.

Smith has a legitimate argument. And you probably do, too, for some of the great numbers through the
years that are just as memorable. Rosenthal mentions
511, the number of pitcher Cy Young's victories in his
perspective, yet 511 is omitted from the distinguished
dozen in this book.

Why? To cite a few reasons, Young won 72 games
in his first three years, beginning in 1890, when the dis-
tance between home plate and the mound was 50 feet,
as opposed to 60 feet, six inches today. He pitched in a
dead ball era when the hitting was so bad and the
strike zones so large, Young easily surpassed 40 starts a
season and even started at least 50 games a few seasons early in his career. This is not meant to demean
the career of a great pitcher, but to point out that 511
is a bit skewed.

However, from the same dead ball era, the Chicago
Cubs record of 116 wins is included. No matter if the
ball was dead or not, a baseball team that pulls together
to win that many games in a 152-game season is
remarkable. (Cy Young proved to be human that year
for the Boston Red Sox, finishing with a 13-21 record
to lead the American League in losses). Not until 1954
did a team challenge the Cubs' record when the
Cleveland Indians set an American League record with
111 wins. The trouble is, neither the Cubs nor the
Indians won the World Series during their record-set-

ting years. That's why the '98 New York Yankees stirred up debate on the greatest teams of all time. Not only did the Yankees surpass the Indians' A.L. record with 114 wins, they won the World Series.

A championship effort in any sport can elevate a team to elite status, but nowhere near the level of excellence achieved by the 1972 Miami Dolphins, a team that could rightfully call itself perfect after a 17-0 season. Yet, from the view of former Dolphins linebacker Nick Buoniconti, the '72 Dolphins still find themselves defending their achievement.

While on the subject of perfection, the '72 Dolphins are a perfect example of that association between a number and an athlete, or in this case, a team of athletes. Say "17-0" and surely you will get a knee-jerk response about that great Dolphin team.

Another famous football number is 47, but it could go two ways. I asked a friend to think about the number 47 in football and his response was Johnny Unitas. No, not his jersey number because he donned number 19 on his back, but the number of consecutive games in which Unitas threw a touchdown pass. It was a great answer to my question, and it could fall into the sacred record category of standing the test of time, but "47" in this book is the winning streak the Oklahoma Sooners strung together in the 1950s when they dominated college football. During that stretch, the Sooners were perfect for three straight seasons under Coach Bud Wilkinson.

Why not 2,105? Eric Dickerson's single-season rushing record in 1984? One could argue that it's a memorable football number, breaking O.J. Simpson's one-season total of 2,003. The only question is whether Dickerson, a member of the Pro Football Hall of Fame, will see his name erased by an up-and-coming running back in college, or by someone already in the NFL. Other records could be cited for their omission from this book, like Walter Payton's all-time rushing record of 16,726 yards. But it doesn't have that special ring to it.

Payton's record sounds more like an answer to the trivia question - How many whiskers are on a man's face?

Another arguable question. What number has more of a ring than 100, signifying the number of points Wilt Chamberlain scored in one game? Can't dispute that. But Wilt's not alone. Although done in college, Frank Selvy scored 100 points in a game for Furman in 1954. And, since we've dipped into the college ranks, how can "7" be omitted as the number of consecutive NCAA basketball titles won by the Bruins? Seven vs. 88. That question is dealt with in this book from two different perspectives.

The perspectives come from figures covering different generations and different angles. Steve Palermo shares the umpire's view of the Ripken streak. Ed Randall shares the Nolan Ryan strikeout record from the view of a fan who grew up watching the Mets in the 60s, then covering all sports as a broadcaster/writer.

You may not agree with the records included (or excluded) but if you're left thinking about them and their perspectives before debating their merits with your buddies, then the goal of this book will have been accomplished.

Enjoy.

Sacred Records

Perspectives

On The

Records

That Have Shaped

Sports

History

1

17-0

The 1972 Miami Dolphins' Perfect Season

The Inside View

Nick Buoniconti

As a member of the 1972 Miami Dolphins team that completed a perfect 17-0 season, former linebacker Nick Buoniconti shares an inside perspective of the prevailing feeling among his comrades as they closely watch any team that dares match the Dolphins' accomplishment. In particular, the ex-Dolphins kept their eyes on the 1985 Chicago Bears and the 1998 Denver Broncos as each went deep into the season unbeaten before falling short of what Miami achieved. Buoniconti, these days, is busy during the NFL season as one of the hosts of HBO's Inside the NFL.

17-0

It's not an attitude as much as a feeling, the feeling being that here you are, a team that did something in NFL history, going undefeated, 17-0, culminating with a Super Bowl win over Washington. It lasted 13 years before the Bears came up and challenged it. Heck, it was like having your manhood attacked. It's something you feel strongly about. Not too many people in the NFL have an accomplishment like that to point to and I think, especially when you accomplish something like that as a team, it's even more of an incredible record.

Whenever someone is approaching that, none of us are happy and, quite candidly, we like to see that team get beat. The Bears took it on the chin and so did Denver.

In '85, I wasn't on the sideline. I was in Cleveland doing a show for *Inside the NFL*. I know what my feeling was because I was watching that game by myself in my hotel room. I sat there and, I have to tell you, I was just fit to be tied because I knew how great a defense that Bears team had. And the Dolphins were not a real good football team that year. They did have some great receivers though. As soon as I saw (Dan) Marino go to a three-step drop and start throwing those slants, I said, "We got them!" (Mark) Clayton and (Mark) Duper were running those slants. They finally figured how to beat Buddy Ryan's 46-Defense. I just felt great. My stomach was in my mouth the whole game, but on the other hand I felt very confident.

I always feel like we end up being the victim. Every time someone challenges our record it seems like we have to defend it. It's something that just happened - we were the beneficiaries of great play.

When the New York Giants were playing Denver (Dec. 13, 1998) I was listening to the game because I was riding in a car on my way to the airport so I could fly down to Miami for the Jets game that same night. As I was listening to the last two or three plays of that game, I had the driver stop. I had to get out of the car. I couldn't listen to the last play because I said, "Oh no, here's John Elway. The fourth quarter. Elway has won so many games miraculously coming from behind." I was walking on the tarmac of the airport and, finally, the driver said, "You can come in now. The Giants won." It was just so nerve-shattering. I was thrilled the Giants won because I felt, if Denver went down to Miami (the Broncos next game on Dec. 21) undefeated, they had all the incentive in the world to win that football game. I think they would have reacted differently than they did with one loss.

There is more emphasis now and the media jumps on it so much more than when we had an undefeated streak going. I think it's played up so much that the team they're playing begins to really focus on that. When the Broncos went to play the Giants, the Giants were really intent. I know because I went out there and talked with those guys and I talked with (Coach) Jim Fassel. They said, "Look, we aren't going to just let them throw their hats on the field and declare a victory. If they're going to win, they're going to have to beat us." They were determined. As a team builds an undefeated record and moves toward 16-0, I think they're facing spirited teams who have pride and determination. They are not going to be the victims that allow this team to go undefeated. In the NFL, not much separates the great teams from the good ones or the bad ones. One or two players can do that.

If we looked at the last few games we played in the regular season, we won pretty handily. Even though the other teams were out there trying to knock us off, I think that we had a much better football team. It's much more difficult to go undefeated now than when we went undefeated simply because of free agency, salary cap problems and not having, because of the salary cap, the good back-up players that you were able to accumulate and stockpile back when we played. Like when Bob Griese went down, we had Earl Morrall or when someone else got hurt, we had someone to step in there. If a team does go undefeated, they certainly deserve it.

I was at the Dolphins-Broncos game. I had already made plans with a bunch of the old Dolphins - Earl Morrall, Bob Griese, Mercury Morris, Jim Kiick and Dick Anderson. That was the game I told Dick Anderson, "Don't forget to bring the Dom Perignon." Every time all the undefeated teams have a loss, we break out a bottle of champagne and we toast the '72 undefeated team. That night, it wasn't just he and I, it was about a half-dozen guys. It was just wonderful.

I talked with (Coach) Denny Green of Minnesota and asked him, "Did you ever think back to that Tampa Bay game the Vikings' lost on Nov. 1?" Because they were 15-1 in the regular season. He said, "Nick, I just don't think anybody is going to go 16-0. I think it's almost impossible." Most people don't understand how difficult it is to go undefeated.

We surprised people. (Coach Don) Shula's first year was in '70 and we were 10-4 (after finishing 3-10-1 in '69). By '72, we were going undefeated. We were an expansion team from '66 that all of a sudden showed up and started winning. We were way down in Miami, way down south. Had we been in New York, Chicago or L.A., or any of the major media markets, every time someone challenged that record people would be talking about how great that '72 football team was instead of us having to defend it.

We were a great football team with a group of great football players. If you look at our record in the three years that we went to Super Bowls (44-6-1 in '71-

'72-'73), very few teams would have ever accomplished that. We were 32-2 over two years (in '72 and '73). That's a heckuva record. I don't think people have given us enough credit and I don't think they understand the magnitude of going undefeated - what it means in the history books of the NFL. It has to be, in my mind, the greatest record in the history of the NFL. There are a lot of individual records, but I don't know of another team record that's more important than that one.

The "No Name Defense" certainly had a lot of great players on it. The no name is really a misnomer. One thing I can tell you, our team was not an over-achieving one. That's signified by the number of guys who have gone into the Hall of Fame on the offensive side. On the defensive side, none of us has gone in yet, but somewhere along the line the media - or whoever selects the Hall of Fame - will recognize that the defense, which set an NFL record for the fewest number of points allowed, deserves to have representation in the Hall of Fame. Maybe the way to do it is to induct the entire defense.

The Outside View

Clay Latimer

Clay Latimer *has covered the sports beat for the* Rocky Mountain News *in Denver since 1982. He was on the Broncos beat when they captured their first Super Bowl win in 1998. Latimer also went inside the life of the Broncos quarterback in the book* John Elway: Armed and Dangerous. *Latimer is frank with his perspective of the Dolphins' perfect season despite knowing the sensitivity of the ex-Dolphins from the '72 team toward any critic that questions their greatness.*

17-0

The '72 Dolphins were a marvelous, well-coached, even inspiring bunch. They were also a freak occurrence, a one-time convergence of time and circumstance, an anomaly rather than a team for the ages. In fact, they weren't even the best team of the '70s.

In 1989, NFL Films and ESPN picked 20 of the best teams since World War II and staged a computerized tournament. The four finalists were the '78 Steelers, '84 49ers, '76 Raiders and the '72 Dolphins. In the semis the Steelers beat the 49ers, 20-17, and the Dolphins defeated the Raiders, 24-21. In the grand finale, the Steelers beat Coach Don Shula's team, 21-20, on the strength of some spectacular goal-line defense and Franco Harris' 3-yard run on the last play.

If ESPN and the NFL staged a computerized tournament today, the Dolphins might not even be among the four finalists. If they staged a computerized season, the Dolphins might not even win 12 games. In 1972, for example, the Dolphins played 14 regular season games and three playoff contests; in 1997, the Broncos played 16 games in the regular season and four playoff games. That adds up to four more chances for defeat - or injuries and other season-ending mishaps. In 1972, the Dolphins played only a handful of teams with winning records.

In the '90s, only a handful of teams can't beat the top teams. In fact, from the salary cap, to the draft, to the waiver-wire, to compensatory draft picks, to pass-blocking rules, to illegal chucking, to hands-off quarterbacks - everything is obsessively geared to competitive balance.

Also, in 1972, Shula could work in relative isolation. But in the predatory 90s, a coach has to fill luxury suites, master free agency, work the multimedia - and at least make a spirited run for the Super Bowl. "We know the risk factors for heart disease: cholesterol, diabetes, high blood pressure, family history, cigarette smoking," Dr. Charles Harrison, the Falcon's team physician, told the Atlanta media following Coach Dan Reeves' heart attack. "I'm going to add another one - NFL coaching - even though it's not listed in the heart books."

The pressure is passed down to players, who often feel like specimens on a microscopic slide, especially when they begin to make a run at perfection. The pressure starts with the press, which is as different from its 70s brethren as a typewriter is from a lap top. "The pressure is so relentless in the NFL in any season," Denver quarterback John Elway said. "But when you're shooting for a perfect season, and every team is shooting at you - it's so mentally draining. And the questions never stop."

"I remember that even after we'd won 10 straight games, there was no national press at our doorstep," wide receiver Paul Warfield said of his '72 team. "Today, after a team wins six, seven games, the national media leans on every word a player says. Maybe that was our saving grace."

Coaches and players have dueled with reporters from day one. It's part of the ol' give-and-take. Mean Joe Greene, for example, once spit in a reporter's face. Jim McMahon blew his nose on a scribe. A Houston reporter got in a verbal tussle with Oilers quarterback Dan Pastorini, who promptly pushed the reporter through a half-open door leading to a practice field. They each landed at the feet of Oilers coach Bum Phillips, who had been telling an interviewer how well his team got along with the media.

But in the 90s, it's really gotten ugly. With the spread of talk radio, cable and a 24-hour news cycle, the press corps resembles a Roman legion - and it's just as militant.

In some cities, television cameras take pictures of newspaper photographers taking pictures of reporters interviewing coaches, who have a bird's eye view of the media bazaar. It takes a small communications army just to handle the throng of electronic reporters, creating a small forest of satellite dishes, antenna and bombast. Players and coaches expose their entire lives to scrutiny - like politicians.

No need to tell ex-Dallas Cowboys coach Barry Switzer. When he twice ordered Emmitt Smith to go up the middle on fourth-and-a-foot - and Smith twice failed - Switzer was assailed by the telegentsia, including Joe Gibbs, Jimmy Johnson, and Mike Ditka, who called it "dumb and dumber."

Coaches bristle at the mention of talk shows. Mad Dog, Berserk Bob, The Truth and the rest of the gang often get more airtime than the Governor does. "When I go to work I either have a CD playing or a phone conversation going," said ex-Kansas City coach Marty Schottenheimer, who took the talk out of radio.

Although their listnership is relatively minuscule, many coaches believe reporters get the pulse of the public from listening to talk radio. "The media listens to the mood of the guy from Squawkie Canyon, who is mad because his coach doesn't know what to call on fourth down," Rich Brooks told *The Sporting News* when he was still the head coach of the Rams. "Maybe this guy doesn't know if the ball is pumped or stuffed, but he talks for 20 minutes, and suddenly what he says is taken as truth."

Players get burned on the talk show hot seat, too. In Miami, a radio station imitated linebacker Bryan Cox's voice making outrageous and personal statements that drove Cox's children home crying from school. And the station was the Dolphins' flagship station. Fans are also more disruptive than ever. "Herman Moore made a great catch in a game and fans were yelling,

'Way to go Herman!'" Ex-Detroit coach Wayne Fontes said. "Thirty seconds later, he comes across the field and drops a routine ball and I hear, 'Fire the coach.'"

In the face of all this pressure, which the '72 Dolphins only fleetingly encountered, modern-era teams are bound to stumble at least once. If they'd faced similar heat in '72, the Dolphins would've certainly lost their way a couple times. Better teams did in ensuing years. In 1990, for example, the San Francisco 49ers had won 10 straight games and 18 in a row dating back to the previous season. By beating the inept Los Angeles Rams (3-7 entering that game) they would break the consecutive win streak they shared with the Chicago Bears of 1933-34 and 1941-42 and the Dolphins of 1972-73, and clinch another NFC West title. Then the 49ers would turn their attention to a mega-Monday night showdown with the New York Giants, who also were unbeatable; it was billed as the Game of the Century.

But it literally rained on the 49ers parade. A weekend downpour turned Candlestick Park into a quagmire. On three consecutive plays in the first quarter, the 49ers and Rams gave the ball back to one another on fumbles and an interception. Three plays after that, 49ers fullback Tom Rathman fumbled, setting up the Rams' first score. In the final quarter, the Rams drove nearly the length of the field. With 2:01 left, Cleveland Gary, the NFL's leading fumbler among backs, fumbled at the 1. "The ball popped out and we dove for it," said Matt Millen, a 49ers linebacker. "The kid got back up after being hit and tried to pick it up. The ball literally went around him and he got it around him and picked it up again and ran for a touchdown. It looked like something from a movie. Sometimes in a game you see something happen and you just say: 'That's it. That's the game.' Well, that was one of those games. The football gods were against us that day."

Bloody Sunday didn't end there. The 10-0 Giants unraveled during a 31-13 loss to the Philadelphia Eagles in another one-day meltdown.

In 1991, the Dallas Cowboys were in takeoff stage, thanks to a solid-gold draft from the previous spring. Yet few knew at that point, which is why the Cowboys were heavy underdogs against the 11-0 Redskins.

Coach Jimmy Johnson knew the Cowboys had a chance if they could avoid playing it safe. A couple of days before the game, he yanked 6-foot-5, 285-pound John Gesek from a group of players and told his team: "If you're going to fight a big gorilla," pointing at Gesek, "and you can't run away, you don't barely hit him. You hit him as hard as you can hit anything. That's what we're going to do Sunday. We're going to go after them with everything."

The Cowboys did just that. Although eight rookies received extended playing time, the Cowboys went for it four times on fourth down, tried an onside kick, blitzed Redskins quarterback Mark Rypien twice as much as they normally would, and repeatedly threw in Pro Bowl cornerback Darrell Green's direction. Quarterback Troy Aikman threw deep on the first play, a 39-yard completion to the Redskins' 24. On the final play of the half, he heaved a Hail Mary scoring pass to rookie Alvin Harper, despite the fact he was 0-for-6 in Hail Mary's. The Cowboys led for good en route to a 24-21 win.

"You know what was even worse than losing that game," said Millen, who had moved over to the Redskins that season. "Losing after we'd knocked out their best player - Aikman. We knocked him out and Steve Beuerlein beat us. It was an ambush, against a division rival, which is when those games often happen."

"It can't be challenged," Mercury Morris said of the Dolphin mark. "Now there will be so much pressure and attention, somebody will set the agenda to knock you off."

No team had a better shot at Miami's record than the 1985 Chicago Bears. Their only loss that year to the Dolphins was after they'd been sidetracked by the side show. At the height of his powers, Jim McMahon could offend anyone with his wicked tongue - even his mother. "By the time Jim grows up, I'll be 6-feet under," Roberta McMahon said that season.

At the Super Bowl, McMahon's headbands, head butts, acupuncture needles, sunglasses, and bare rear end became front-page news around the globe. But the Bears had broken new ground well before then. In fact, by mid-December, McMahon and Co. had already released their wild stomping "Super Bowl Shuffle." William "The Fridge" Perry was running roughshod over NFL decorum and Coach Mike Ditka had long since given up on reigning in his Bad News Bears.

While the Bears were doing *Entertainment Tonight*, Shula was laying a dangerous trap. In the Miami locker room, 1972's veterans pleaded with the '85 Dolphins to preserve their perfection. Wired fans charged the electric air at Joe Robbie Stadium. The noise was unbearable. The Bears never had a chance to adapt to their scary surroundings. They were more concerned about figuring out the Dolphin offense.

The Dolphins jumped to a 31-10 halftime lead and won 38-24. In 1998, after the Broncos finished with a 17-2 record, and their second consecutive Super Bowl title, can anybody seriously argue that the '72 Dolphins were a superior team? Were they any better than the Dallas Cowboys' great 90s teams? Or the Packers? DiMaggio's record is timeless; the Dolphins' is not. They were a team of their time, but not all time.

70

2

Mark McGwire's Single Season Home Run Record

The Bird's Eye View
Mike Shannon

F
*ormer St. Louis Cardinals outfielder-third base-
man Mike Shannon knew Roger Maris as well as
anybody. As teammates, after Maris was traded
from the New York Yankees to the Cardinals in
December, 1966, before the pennant winning season
in '67, they became close. Shannon was chosen by the
Maris family as one of the pallbearers after Maris died
of cancer in 1985. As a member of the radio team of
the St. Louis Cardinals in 1998, Shannon was the only
broadcaster to witness first-hand each of the 70 home
runs blasted by Mark McGwire. McGwire surpassed
the single-season record formerly held since 1961 by
one of Shannon's best friends. Shannon shares his perspective of McGwire's historic march to a record that
captured America's attention.*

70

As far as I'm concerned, the first and most important thing about Mark McGwire's entire season is that on the Friday of the last weekend he was not leading the National League in home runs. He had 65 home runs. Sammy Sosa had 66.

McGwire hit two on that Friday night, he hit one on Saturday and he hit two more on Sunday. That's five home runs in the last three games. To show you what a true champion he is and what kind of a competitor he is, that was big time pressure. Nobody really talked about it.

If you're Mark McGwire, and you're sitting in your hotel room, you're saying to yourself, "Man, here I've had the greatest season ever. I've broken Roger Maris' single season home run record and I'm not even leading the National League and I might not lead the league in home runs. I'm one behind." And he went out and did what he did. To me, that put everything on top. The cherry. The whipped cream.

I enjoyed watching the people enjoy the season. I've never seen baseball fans enjoy a season like they enjoyed the 1998 season. They would get to the ballpark and stand outside, waiting for the gates to open so they could see this man take batting practice.

If he didn't hit the ball out of the ballpark in batting practice, they booed him. They booed the batting practice pitcher if he threw one out of the strike zone. I wanna tell you, that's also some big time pressure. There would be 100, 200 or 300 of the media standing behind home plate just waiting for him. It seemed like the whole world stopped when he got into the batting cage. Maybe when the game started, all the pressure was off.

So many things. One time, he got a base hit down in Miami. I mean, he hit a rocket line drive and they booed him because it was only a single and he just laughed about it. In my opinion, it is a year that will never be duplicated. Never.

I never did think that McGwire would break the record because I thought the pressure would get to him in the media. Because Sosa and McGwire were playing off one another, that kind of nullified all that pressure. When there are two of them, and with all that's going on, there are so many things that can be answered. The pressure is really cut to one-tenth of what it would be if there was one guy and he was an island out there.

They fed off of one another. How about the game in Chicago (Aug. 19)! Sosa hits the home run and moves ahead of McGwire. In the eighth inning, McGwire hits a home run to tie him and tie the game, then McGwire hits another home run in the 11th inning to win it. That was his 49th home run of the year.

You have to remember that McGwire went to spring training wanting to hit 50 home runs. We went to New York the day after he hit his 49th. There were 20,000 people out there for batting practice. Naturally, there was more press than ever. Bingo! What did he do? He hits number 50 that night. It was like a Hollywood script. I just shook my head. He couldn't believe it either. Trust me.

There's no doubt he was capable of it. As a Cardinal, in his first 162 games, he hit 71 home runs. He knew that and everyone knew that, but to do that in one year is a different thing. I think he knew everything was in place when he went into spring training, but I don't think anyone had any idea that Sosa was going to push him like that. Everybody thought it would be (Ken) Griffey, Jr.

He hit his 61st on his dad's 61st birthday, then he came right back the next night and hit his 62nd. It was really nice the way all that happened. It was nice for the Maris kids to be there because, after all, they were losing something. That record was them. You have to know the Maris family. I mean, they're very close and very protective. I know they thought having the record broken was going to hurt and it really didn't. They got to where they enjoyed it. They saw what a nice person Mark is and they knew what a nice person their father was.

I said, "Look, if your dad were here today, who do you think he would pick to break the record? Who do you think he would like to pass the torch to?" I think it's very simple. It would have been Mark McGwire even though Sosa was having a good year too. McGwire is a Cardinal and Roger was a Cardinal.

Roger and I became very good friends - I considered him my best friend. By the time he became a Cardinal, all the fanfare surrounding his record was gone. By then, he really didn't have an outlet to share his feelings about the record. It's hard to talk to your family about that, or to anybody except for one of your peers. I never once asked him anything about the record, he just started talking and I listened. It was a thrill for me, but what he was really doing was venting. I was just fortunate to be the guy who was there at the right time, the right place. We played golf together, we fished together, we hunted together. Our family got along. The kids got along. Our wives got along. It was really an unbelievable friendship all the way around.

Knowing Roger the way I knew him, my only wish is that he could have been there in '98. And I'm sure he was. I'm sure he was there watching. Mark said he felt Roger was with him in many ways.

It all started when the young Maris boys came to me and asked if they could meet Mark. They came into Atlanta because they live in Florida and it was close. That's really how it got started with Mark and Roger because they really didn't know much about one another.

Tony LaRussa (the Cardinals' manager) was very instrumental in that meeting. I arranged it so that we went to the ballpark early to see Tony. He brought them into his office, then he went out and got "Big Mac" and I introduced everybody. I stayed around for about a minute or two and when I saw everything was going well I left. They had a really nice meeting, for 20 or 30 minutes, then they went into the dugout and watched everything.

That took some pressure off of him, too. The Maris kids got to know him and he got to know the Maris family. Roger would have been so thrilled to see that because of the way everyone was pulling for McGwire. No one pulled for Roger. It wasn't his fault. If McGwire was where Roger was in '61, he would have been in the same boat. They would have been booing him (McGwire).

McGwire and Maris have so much in common. Both, very nice people. They'd give you the shirt off their back. Good family guys. Good citizens. It just goes on and on. If you took their swings, their hands and their arms, and took the rest of their bodies away, you wouldn't be able to tell them apart. From the starting position, through hitting the baseball, almost identical. Mark has a little bigger swing because he takes that top hand off the bat where Roger didn't always do that. As far as being short and compact, it's just unbelievable. When you see film of Roger swinging from the left side, just watch the way he swings. Both have a little upper cut. It's scary when you analyze them. Not many people look at it that way because Mark's physique is so different from Roger's. But Roger was also very strong. He could pull the outside pitch better than anyone I ever saw. Maris could take a ball six to eight inches outside and pull it foul past first base.

You have to remember that Babe Ruth was the God of Baseball. No one wanted him dethroned. No one at all. Not the public. Not the Yankees. No one. Roger didn't set out to break the record. Roger set out to hit more home runs than Mickey (Mantle). The year before, he (Maris) was the Most Valuable Player, but Mickey still got all the ink. Roger said, "Well, I was the Most Valuable Player, but I was still the whipping boy and Mickey was still the fair-haired kid. It must be the home runs." He made up his mind in December of '60 that he was going to hit more home runs. He decided that for himself; he didn't tell anybody about it. He was a strong-willed German. When he made up his mind to do something, you could bet that it was going to be accomplished. He was funny the way he told me, "He'd hit one and I'd hit one. He'd hit one and I'd hit two."

They went into July and August neck and neck, then got into September in the 50s, but Mickey dropped back and Roger went on. You can't believe the amount of pressure that was on him. First of all, the Yankees gave him no protection. What I mean by no protection is he stayed in the hotel and they didn't put him under an assumed name. They didn't give him another room. No protection. No security. Nothing.

And the press. They never made any arrangements for the press, so if there were 200, 300, 400 or 500 of the press at the ballpark, Roger talked to almost every one of those guys. I mean, you're talking about hours after a game. That's the kind of thing he went through for months.

The world was coming down on this guy and all he wanted to do was play baseball. All he wanted to do was go out and do something good. Roger was smart enough and worldly enough to know it was just the situation.

The only guy who pitched to him was (Tracy) Stallard with the 61st home run. You had to appreciate and know Tracy because he couldn't have slept with himself if he didn't try to pitch to him. Roger told me the last nine or 10 home runs, besides Stallard's pitches, were all on pitches out of the strike zone. I don't think anyone other than Roger Maris, under those circumstances, could have done what he did.

What McGwire did in '98 is just as phenomenal as Maris' feat in '61. I don't think it distracts at all from what Roger did because what he did, at that particular time, was something everyone had to take their hats off to. Especially "Big Mac." There are only a few guys who know how all of us feel. McGwire is definitely one of them. You can see the kind of appreciation that they have for one another though they never knew each other. Also, Roger didn't know Babe Ruth, but I guarantee you, when they're all up there in heaven, they're going to have a helluva time talking about all this. You might have to throw in Sosa, (Ralph) Kiner and a couple of other guys who got close.

I kept telling people on the broadcast, "Please, buy the tickets now. You can see it coming in September and you don't want to miss it because it might never, ever happen again."

What was more phenomenal about it is that every time the fans came to the ballpark, it seemed like this guy delivered. I interviewed him almost every time a big home run came and would look at him and say, "Mark, it's not that easy!"

For Ruth's era and what he did, he has got to be the greatest baseball player ever. When you look and see what Babe Ruth did, when he did it, hands down the greatest player ever. He was hitting 50 home runs when the rest of the league combined was hitting about 60. When he hit 60 home runs, he had as many as five teams combined! I mean, this guy was so far ahead of his time that it was unbelievable.

This guy is the greatest home run hitter ever. He is so far ahead of everyone else. I didn't get to see Ruth, but George Kissell, who has been in our organization and has known the game since the 20s, will list them for you. Just for brute strength, hitting the ball a long way and vicious swings, McGwire is at the top and, he says, by a large margin. He has Ruth and Josh

Gibson on that list. When you see what McGwire is doing now, and how far he hits the ball, that's what so amazing. He hits the ball where the ball has never been hit before. In that respect, this guy is going to go down as the greatest home run hitter ever if he stays healthy. Tony LaRussa thinks he's going to hit 75. If he hits 75, I'm going to retire or think about it, I'll tell you that. Unbelievable!

The Locker Room View
Mark McGwire

*T*ypically, during his record-setting 1998 season when Mark McGwire finished as the single season home run king, he held a news conference for road games before the first game of the series. The following passage is a condensed first person account from McGwire at a Sept. 18 news conference, before the start of a weekend series in Milwaukee. By then, McGwire had already eclipsed the Maris record and was still in a furious race down the wire with Sammy Sosa before opening up daylight on the final weekend. Little did he know that an umpire's ruling that weekend would take away an apparent home run that would have ultimately given him 71 homers on the year. At the news conference, the opening question to McGwire was, "How important is it to finish first in the home run race?"

70

I don't think it really matters. I think what he and I have been doing is fantastic. I mean, what we've done, nobody in the game has done for 37 years and I'm pretty happy with the way things have been going.

All I did was swing a bat. What happened to me the night that I broke it (the record) is fantastic. I don't think it needs to be made up to a big deal that I got something (like a car).

Like I've been saying since day one, it comes down to getting pitches to hit and putting a good swing on it. I know everybody is trying to analyze, "Well, they face this pitching staff and this team. He's (Sosa) in the playoff hunt; He's (McGwire) not in the playoff hunt." Throw it out the door. It comes down to getting pitches to hit. If you get 'em and put good swings on 'em, there's a good chance you might get a hit. It doesn't mean it's going to be a home run. I mean, sometimes I think people are sitting there going, "Well, they're at 63. They haven't hit something in a couple of days. What's wrong with them?" My God, give me a break. Let's just enjoy what's going on instead of trying to critique everything that's not going on.

I've said since day one, "There's a pitcher on the mound. I see the best every day and he's trying to get me out. He's not going to set it on a tee for me. Period."

I think the thing that I'm trying to get across is that I enjoy playing the game. I love the game dearly. I play hard every day. I work hard at what I do. I don't know how much else you want to do. Somebody is going to sit there and say, "This guy's a role model because of the numbers he puts up." I think a role model is a person who has lived his life right. I think everybody on this earth makes mistakes, but people who are role models are the ones who overcome the mistakes and become good people because of them.

I don't think anybody in this world will ever know what Sammy and me have gone through. There are only three people - Roger Maris, Sammy Sosa and Mark McGwire. I don't think anybody out there has a concept of what we've gone through and it's not easy. Believe me.

We have a good understanding of each other and we respect each other tremendously. I mean, here are two guys from two different countries who have great sportsmanship, really admire each other, really pull for each other and if there's anything that's good for the game that comes out of this, it's to see that. To see the sportsmanship of two athletes who are talented, who can come together and really enjoy each other, and what they do.

I'll probably never tell the story. I'll probably just keep it to myself. It's a mental grind. This whole game is a mental grind.

If you're going to tell that story, you're going to write a book and I'm so dead set against writing a book. As far as I'm concerned, I'll never write a book while I'm playing. And the chances of writing a book when I'm retired are probably slim to none. I just don't believe in that.

It's not going to change my life. I've said since day one, "It's the people around you who change." I've already seen people change around me. People look at you in a different way. They want to touch you. They want to shake your hand. They want to say that they've said, "Hi!" to you. It's just weird how, because of something you do, people look at you differently and I've come from a family that (believes) you never put anybody on a pedestal. Everybody's the same.

People are talented and they're given a certain thing by the Man upstairs to do on this earth. It just so happens that I'm a baseball player and I've worked hard at what I'm doing, but I just wish people wouldn't change around me.

What do I want them (his future grandchildren) to remember? One helluva year, I'll tell that. One helluva year just because of the expectations going into the new year and into spring training. The talk of it, and all of a sudden you reach it, you break it. Then Sammy does it. What a great year!

Records can be broken. Put your mind to it. Work hard. Records can be broken.

3

4,256

Pete Rose's All-Time Hit Record

The Southern Gentleman's View
Ernie Harwell

ike Ty Cobb, Ernie Harwell is a Georgia native. Enshrined in the broadcasters wing of the Baseball Hall of Fame in Cooperstown, N.Y., Harwell has entertained generations of fans as a play-by-play voice, predominantly in Detroit, where he started in 1960 as a Tiger broadcaster. As one who has seen and met many of the greats in baseball, both on the field and those who preceded his broadcasting career, Harwell offers his view of Pete Rose's all-time record of 4,256 hits, which surpassed the previous record, 4,191, held by Cobb, the Georgia Peach.

4,256

Everybody can focus and zero in on those numbers and understand exactly what they mean. You can just say the number and people immediately identify with it. That doesn't happen in other sports. Numbers in other sports just don't seem to have that significance.

Plus, baseball started so much longer ago than any other sport that it has developed a tradition over the years that can't be touched by the more recent sports like football and basketball. Professional football and basketball came along a lot later than baseball. I think part of baseball's appeal is the tradition and the lore. The fact that it goes from generation to generation also helps us recognize those numbers.

The most unbreakable record of all time is Johnny Vandermeer's double no-hit performance. I don't see anybody pitching three consecutive no-hit games. The McGwire record is, of course, outstanding and probably has more glamour and appeal than any other. Everybody loves the home runs.

I think the Joe DiMaggio record of 56 straight games in which he hit safely is a tremendous record because it takes a day-by-day performance and concentration - the ability to get at least one hit per game, which is not easy. On the home run record, for instance, you could miss a home run for a week or two and probably make it up, but on a record like DiMaggio's, you just can't falter in one game.

I thought Cobb's record would stand forever because he played a long time. He was a great hitter. He hit .367 lifetime. He was also the number one base

stealer of all time. Before Babe Ruth came along, Ty
Cobb was baseball's number one performer. Ty had set
his record back in the late 20s and most of the people
who were there to see it, or read about it, or hear about
it weren't even around when Pete Rose finally eclipsed
the mark. That negated any feeling that people had of
not wanting Pete Rose to break Ty Cobb's record.

I interviewed Cobb quite a few times, wrote some
magazine pieces about him. Also, I was the emcee at
various luncheons that he attended. He was always
very good to me but he had a reputation of being oth-
erwise when he played. Certainly by the time I met
him I think he had mellowed. My association with him
was very pleasant.

Of course, he died long before Pete Rose came
along with the record-breaking performance that he
put up. I guess Cobb felt like that record never would
be busted.

Sparky Anderson (the former Reds manager) has
told me many, many times that when he had Pete, he'd
see him take batting practice after a game. He'd hit until
his hands bled. He was just the consummate hustler, a
guy who bore down all the time and did everything he
could to make himself better. Sparky said there were a
lot of players that probably had more ability, but Pete
was able to get the most out of what he had.

To break the record, I think it would take somebody with longevity, somebody who stays around a
long time and plays almost every game each year,
maybe for 20 to 25 years and avoids injuries. That's
one of the big bugaboos. It can be done. I think it's
going to be harder, although the players today seem to
be better conditioned and seem to last longer. Maybe
because they are better conditioned or maybe because
the money is there, they'll want to keep playing.

There's more pressure on players because of
greater media attention. You've got ESPN, you've got
the talk shows and you've got instant television. In the
days of Ty Cobb, you played a game in the afternoon

and nobody knew what happened until it was in the paper the next morning. Now everything's instantaneous and so blown out of proportion that I think it puts a lot of extra pressure on the players.

If someone were to challenge the record, he'd have to be able to handle the situation. I think he would have to be somebody like George Brett, or Mark McGwire, or maybe Sammy Sosa. I think (Ken) Griffey, Jr. could probably handle it. Another player who comes to mind is Paul Molitor. I thought he was level-headed. He and Robin Yount were a couple guys who could have handled something like that. Molitor had a shot at DiMaggio's record and I think he handled it very well, but it's a long way to 56 games. Certain other guys wouldn't be able to take that pressure. They wouldn't react to the media the way they'd have to and it might cause them some problems.

Those numbers, like getting 3,000 hits or winning 20 games, are magic numbers. Thirty would be even more magical. I was lucky to see Denny McLain's 31 victories in 1968. It's getting more rare as we go along. That was the first time since the early 1930s when Dizzy Dean did it. You have to figure, between Dean and McLain, a lot has passed by.

I started broadcasting in the National League. I did six years with Brooklyn and the New York Giants so I got to see, at that point, a lot of the great National League players. I saw Willie Mays break in when I was with the Giants and I was with Brooklyn when Jackie Robinson played. Then I went to the American League in 1954. Later on, one of my big regrets was that I never got to see someone like Roberto Clemente perform except for a World Series or an All-Star game. Now that's been ameliorated, at least to some extent. We can see the National Leaguers through inter-league play with the American League.

Pete Rose. You've got to hand it to him. He stuck around long enough and he was Charlie Hustle. No question about that. I think he deserves the title of the all-time hit leader. He had done everything right. He certainly put up the numbers. I think those records, as they say, are made to be broken. More power to Pete Rose for eclipsing that record.

The Reds View
Joe Nuxhall

J oe Nuxhall broke into the big leagues at the age of 15 as a left-handed pitcher when he made an appearance for the Cincinnati Reds in 1944, then returned to the big leagues in 1952 and stayed in the majors until 1966. Nuxhall was 15-8 as a starter with the Reds in 1963, the year Pete Rose broke into the big leagues. Nuxhall, as a former teammate who saw Rose's traits up close at an early stage to later when broadcasting as a commentator on the Reds radio network, witnessed a historical career unfolding, not only when Rose played for the Reds, but when he played against the Reds. After his playing days were over, Nuxhall threw batting practice to Rose many times after games in spring training. As one who knew him well, Nuxhall offers his perspective on Rose's record of 4,256 hits.

4,256

Right away, you knew he was a hard worker and that he really, in a sense, dedicated himself to becoming a good hitter. I think it was Whitey Ford who put the tag "Charlie Hustle" on him from a spring training game, but that was just his demeanor. His dad was an amateur athlete around Cincinnati and he had the reputation of playing hard at all times. Pete just carried that on.

Particularly in the National League, that "Charlie Hustle" nickname got bigger and bigger because that's what he did. On walks, he ran like they were doubles. Sometimes, I think some of the old veterans back then thought perhaps he was showing them up, but that was just his way of playing the game. There was nothing wrong with it.

When he took extra batting practice, it was always to hit the ball somewhere. He didn't try to hit the ball out of the ballpark like a lot of individuals. He really worked at hitting the ball the opposite way, putting himself in situations - man on second, nobody out, at least get him over. I think that with every swing of the bat he thought, "What am I going to do with this particular swing?" As you watched him progress through his career, you could certainly see how it paid off.

He was a worker. I remember when Sparky (Anderson) decided to put George Foster in left field and Pete at third base. You could ask Russ Nixon, who was one of our coaches then. Pete almost wore Russ out. Russ hit fungoes at third base, particularly before home games. It didn't bother him. He had to work on his fielding and he did that. I threw batting practice many times to him for a half-hour, then he'd go play a ballgame. A lot of times during the season, the team would have extra hitting on the road. If you went out at around 2:00 in the afternoon, nine out of ten times Pete would be there.

(Johnny) Bench and a lot of those guys always wanted extra hitting in spring training, in particular, when the Reds finished playing. It would last a half-hour to 40 minutes. They were, I guess you would say, geared up mentally and felt that was a good time to work. Honestly, I would say that there was no out-and-out pattern to pitch to Pete Rose. As I said, he was not a guy who would swing the bat for home runs. He was dedicated to putting the bat on the ball and letting it land where it might. Consequently, when you get a guy like that, there is basically nowhere you could pitch to him because he had such control of the bat. He studied pitching very hard. Pete could tell you today who is going to pitch next Thursday. I mean, that's the way he approached the game.

If I were pitching to him, I would want to throw him some off-speed stuff. Try to get him out in front as you would pitch to a power hitter because they're really charged up. If you had a good change-up - but not consistently, just on certain occasions - that would have been my way of trying to get Pete out. If you had a good sinking fastball, particularly when he batted left-handed, you kept the ball down and away from him. There again, against the big hitters usually, if you could keep the ball away from them and particularly down, you'd have a shot. That might have been the best way to approach Pete. I'm not saying it would work, but, in my observation of him, I feel that way. I think anybody likes a challenge whether it'd be Pete Rose, or Babe Ruth or Mark McGwire. It's fun to try to outwit them.

I had some success with Stan Musial, Duke Snider

and some of the old-timers. Later in my career, I had some success with Clemente. On Clemente in particular, you just took chances on pitching him certain ways. On any good hitter, I don't think you could pitch him the same all the time. If you do, you're asking for trouble. Clemente was one of those. If you pitched him the same way all the time, he would really get to you. He was a real challenge to pitch to.

I think the best example of Pete, in talking about pressure, was the (44-game) hitting streak. To me, the Ty Cobb thing was fantastic, but you knew it was going to happen. Pete might have approached it that way knowing that he was going to get there. But the hitting streak - every game and every A.B. (at-bat) - really didn't bother him. If it did, he certainly didn't show it. He was a guy who, in my opinion, was relaxed at all times. Joe DiMaggio's 56-game hitting streak is one of the great records in baseball.

To challenge Pete's record, it would have to be a Wade Boggs-type hitter. Or Tony Gwynn. Guys that strike out very few times during the course of the year and are always putting the ball in play. They would certainly be the kind of individuals who would be capable of doing it, but I doubt if it could ever be done because I don't think guys will play that long anymore. With the money factor you might have a few, but I don't think total dedication to the game will be that great as we go on.

Pete always kept himself in good condition, too. Pete took care of himself physically. He worked hard at staying in condition, which certainly helps when it comes to the injury factor.

He was really a fun individual to watch play the game of baseball. He made himself into a good third baseman. He made himself into a good outfielder. He made himself into a good second baseman. He made himself into a good first baseman. All because of his work habits. A lot of guys could say, "Well, I could go over here and I'll take some ground balls and that will be it. I'll go on, take my A.B.'s and forget about it." Well, Pete wasn't like that. He wanted to be the best he could be at any position and certainly it was hitting.

4

56

Joe DiMaggio's Record Hitting Streak

The Penetrative View

George Grande

These days, George Grande is the television voice of the Cincinnati Reds, but when the first ESPN Sportscenter aired on Sept. 7, 1979, Grande was one of the original anchors. In 1980, when ESPN for the first time showed live coverage of the Baseball Hall of Fame induction ceremony, Grande was there. Every year since, Grande returns to Cooperstown for the ceremonies to recognize the returning Hall of Famers on that special weekend. As a former member of the Yankee television broadcast team, Grande is one of only a few in the media who has had the chance to catch Joe DiMaggio in a relaxed moment. He is also one of the few who had the chance to sit down and reminisce with the Yankee Clipper about his career, including DiMaggio's 56-game hitting streak.

56

A sure way to start an argument with any true baseball fan is to initiate a discussion comparing great baseball players from different generations. Who's the greatest home run hitter, Babe Ruth or Henry Aaron? Who's the greatest singles hitter, Ty Cobb or Pete Rose? Is Nolan Ryan a better strikeout pitcher than Bob Feller? The list goes on and on. We all know these are debates that are non-winnable but the exercise is one of sport's greatest lures. The only concrete measure we have to judge these debates are the numbers these athletes put up - be it 714 home runs, 3,000 strikeouts, 2,130 consecutive games or 938 stolen bases. Sometimes those numbers rise above the athletes themselves and live on in the game. One such example is Joe DiMaggio's 56-game hit streak in 1941.

Among all career and single season marks, the Yankee Clipper's consecutive game hit streak remains one of sports most magical statistics and accomplishments. It clearly ranks him as not only one of the best players of his era, but as one of the best to ever play the game. Like Babe Ruth, his aura transcends all he accomplished on the field. To those who played with him or against him and to those who wrote about him or just cheered for him, Joe DiMaggio's legend was even greater than his numbers.

Over the years I have been fortunate to grow close to Yankee greats like Yogi Berra, Phil Rizzuto, Whitey Ford, Mel Allen and most importantly Lefty Gomez. It was through them that I first got a glimpse of the man behind the numbers. It was because of my relationship with them that I had the chance to get to know the Yankee Clipper.

Clearly, Joe DiMaggio was very proud of all he accomplished on the baseball field. He truly believed he was one of the greatest to play the game. At the same time, Joe never liked to toot his own horn. That was never the DiMaggio style. He reveled in the moments he shared with teammates and opponents as they recounted those great Yankee years and he always shined like a light bulb when those men acknowledged his accomplishments as a player and as a man.

With few exceptions, Joe was aloof from his teammates and opponents. One notable exception was Lefty Gomez, the great Yankee pitcher. Not only was Lefty a Hall of Fame pitcher, he was also one of the game's greatest personalities and characters. Lefty was never afraid to poke fun at himself or at any situation that could produce a smile. Joe let down his guard with Lefty because not only did he genuinely like him, he also appreciated his ability to keep his teammates loose.

Never was this relationship more evident, or important, than during Joe's streak of 1941. From the inception of the streak on May 15th to its end on July 17th, Lefty was always there for Joe. Whether it was as a friend to go to dinner with, someone to go out for take-out food, a teammate to talk to in the room, or just someone to take a late night walk with, Lefty was always the man Joe relied on. When fans would close in on Joe at his hotel, it was Lefty who would go down to the lobby and tell them he just saw Joe at a hotel across town. Lefty was the foil Joe needed to keep his life as normal as possible while the streak grew. More than one of Joe's teammates acknowledged to me that had it not been for Lefty, the DiMaggio streak never would have reached its historic proportions.

One of the routines Joe and Lefty had on road trips was to take a cab to the ballpark together each day. Lefty would go downstairs and get a cab set up and Joe would come down a few minutes later rushing past fans and getting right into the waiting cab. What Joe didn't know was that Lefty would always tell the cabby not to talk about the streak because Joe was very superstitious about it. Ironically, the day the streak was stopped in Cleveland, the cabby had ignored Lefty's instructions and brought up the streak. Joe was irritated and got off on the wrong foot. Lefty said he wished he could have put his hands around the cabby's neck!

During the streak, DiMaggio was on fire. In almost half of the games he had multiple hits and for the entire streak he hit .408 (91 for 223). But there were some close calls. Lefty especially remembered one against Philadelphia pitcher John Babich. Babich made it clear he planned to stop the streak and told everyone who would listen. The day before Babich was to pitch, Lefty tried to get Babich to quiet his rhetoric, but to no avail. Even Joe sensed Babich was up to something. Babich's game plan became clear to everyone. The first time up Babich walked Joe on four straight pitches. None near the strike zone. The second time up he threw three straight balls. Again, none near the strike zone. On the fourth delivery, which was again way high and outside, Joe reached out and lashed a line drive right back at Babich through the middle to the infield for a hit that kept the streak alive. The ball nearly hit Babich in the head and, as Lefty described it, silenced him for the remainder of the season.

While fate was with DiMaggio on that day, it was not on the day the streak ended in Cleveland. In his first at-bat, DiMaggio hit a hard shot down the third base line. Indians third baseman Ken Keltner backhanded the grounder and with an off-balance throw just nipped Joe at first for the out. After a walk his second time up, DiMaggio hit another hard ground ball toward the hole between third and short. This time Keltner ranged to his left, gobbled it up and threw DiMaggio out. Either one of those shots could have been a hit on another day, but not on July 17, 1941.

Joe's final at-bat resulted in a double play ground ball to Cleveland shortstop Lou Boudreau. The remarkable 56-game hitting streak had taken its final breath and Kenny Keltner would forever be linked to one of baseball's greatest accomplishments.

Can anyone hit in 56 straight games again? Joe always said, "Sure it can happen, and probably will some day," but frankly I doubt it will ever be matched. Twice in our lifetime athletes have given it a run, but fell far short. Pete Rose hit in 44 straight in 1978 and Paul Molitor in 39 straight in 1987. In this day and age of instant live media coverage, it would be extremely difficult for an athlete to sustain the physical, mental and emotional peak needed to challenge the DiMaggio mark. The most formidable obstacle would be the emotional drain from non-stop media coverage and fan attention. We had a taste of what it would be like in 1998 when Mark McGwire and Sammy Sosa chased and surpassed the single season home run marks of Babe Ruth and Roger Maris. While the pressure on them was immense, they didn't have to get a hit every day as you would to chase DiMaggio's mark.

The only athlete I have ever seen who possessed the ability to withstand that kind of pressure was Pete Rose. Both during his own hitting streak of 44 games in 1978 and his chase of the Ty Cobb all-time hit record, he had the ability not only to deal with the media and fans, but to thrive on it. There aren't many like Pete. To even get in the same neighborhood as Rose, a player would need a great offensive philosophy, patience, knowledge of the strike zone and knowledge of the pitchers he would be facing and, most importantly, good health and good luck.

Yes, Joe DiMaggio's 56-game hitting streak will always live as one of baseball's special gems. It comes with one more footnote.

More than a month after the streak had ended, while the Yankees were in Washington playing the Senators, Joe's close friend Lefty Gomez lured the

Yankee Clipper to a teammate's room presumably to talk about preparations for the World Series because the Yankees had a huge lead over the Red Sox on the way to another American League pennant. When DiMaggio walked into the room he was surprised by the entire team who gave him a champagne toast to honor him for his hitting streak. Gomez had arranged for Tiffany's to engrave a sterling silver cigar humidor with a picture of Joe swinging the bat and an inscription of his 56 game streak. Years later when I asked the Yankee Clipper which one of his many trophies he cherished the most, he said it was that humidor because it came from his teammates.

The Mound View
Eldon Auker

As a 24-year old right-handed pitcher for Detroit, Eldon Auker started Game Seven of the 1934 World Series against the St. Louis Cardinals in the heyday of the Gas House Gang. It was his second season in a 10-year big league career, which included pitching against Babe Ruth and Lou Gehrig as well as Joe DiMaggio who broke into the majors in 1936. While pitching for the St. Louis Browns in 1941, Auker faced DiMaggio during his 56-game hitting streak and shared his thoughts on the Yankee Clipper and the hitting streak that set the standard.

56

There wasn't much talk about it. It was more publicity than anything else. As far as the opposing players were concerned no one really cared whether he broke a record or not. In fact, there has been more made of it recently than there was during the streak. The New York papers played it up a lot.

I had DiMaggio stopped in New York on his 41st. I had him out the first three times, then the next time, he hit a ball off our third baseman's shoulder for a double. If I wanted to stop DiMaggio's streak, all I had to do was walk him or hit him, but I was trying to get him out.

He didn't take a big swing like (Ted) Williams or (Babe) Ruth. He took a swing more like (Lou) Gehrig. Just stood flat-footed and hit it. Gehrig was the same type of hitter except he hit on the left side. He had big legs, you know, and he'd dig in with that left foot and plant that right one. He was just like a stump. DiMaggio was the same way except he had a wider stance. He'd just stand perfectly still and swing through the ball. He had powerful wrists.

Edgar Martinez hits a little like DiMaggio. He just stands perfectly flat-footed, doesn't stride at all. It's like playing golf. They keep their heads down and stand perfectly still. Good hitters just stand there and wait. If they have a good set of wrists, they can do that.

In my career, I hurt my right shoulder while I played football at Kansas State University for Coach Bo McMillin. I guess now it's called a separation; we used to call it a "knockdown." I had a knockdown twice and got muscle bound in it, so I couldn't throw over the top and ended up throwing sidearm when I went into professional baseball. I lost only two games in college in the three years I was eligible to pitch for varsity.

When I signed with the Tigers, they sent me down to Decatur (Ill.) in the Three-I League (Illinois-Iowa-Indiana) and there was a fella named Bob Coleman, who was the manager down there. He watched me throw and he said, "Look, Eldon, if you're going to pitch in the major leagues, you've got to be able to throw the ball over the plate. Most sidearmers have trouble with control. Did you ever try to throw directly underhanded?"

He said, "There was a pitcher for the Yankees years ago by the name of Carl Mays. He threw directly underhanded and had good control. You remind me of him a little bit and I'd like to see if you could try it."

I was pretty fast and had a good curveball, so I pitched batting practice a couple of days fooling around with it.

Quincy (Ill.) was leading the league at that time and they came into town. Coleman said, "Eldon, I want you to pitch this ballgame nine innings underhanded. I don't give a damn how many people you walk or how many hits they get off you. I just want you to pitch nine innings underhanded.

Well, I did. I shut them out and they got two hits, I think, off me. I struck out about 12 or 13 and pitched that way ever since. I pitched for ten years in the major leagues and never had a sore arm in my life.

Ruth didn't like unorthodox pitching. We had a guy on the club (Tigers), a left-handed relief pitcher named Chief Hogsett. He threw sidearmed and three-quarters underhanded and, Christ, Ruth had taken himself out of the ballgame when Chief would come in. Ruth couldn't hit him with a handful of sand. I don't think he ever got a hit off Hogsett in his life.

There are some hitters who don't like unorthodox pitching.

I went to Hofstra University a few years ago when Phil Rizzuto was given a doctorate for humanities by that university. Before Phil went up to the stage, he said to me in the front row, "I want to see you as soon as I get through here." When he finished, he stepped down off the stage and said, "You know, I haven't seen you for years. Did you know that the first time I ever faced you, you hit me in the head with a pitched ball and sent me to the hospital?" I said, "No, I don't remember." He said, "You bounced one off my head and it didn't make me so mad. But it sure upset my mother!"

I had pretty good luck with DiMaggio over the years because he didn't like the unorthodox pitching either. I used to pitch him in on his fists a lot so he couldn't get the good part of his bat on it. If you pitched away from him where he got the good part of the bat on it, he'd hurt you. I tried to keep it in on him and keep it low. He tried to adjust to it and, on this particular day (June 26) in New York, I struck him out twice. He popped up once, then on his last at-bat he hit the ball down and got the double out of it. The last time at-bat.

It's pretty hard for a guy to hit in that many consecutive games. You're up there every day, every day, every day and it's pretty hard to have a good day every day in professional baseball. I've seen some good hitters that never had them (hitting streaks). Charlie Gehringer was a great hitter, but I'd see him hit in only eight or ten straight games, and (Hank) Greenberg, (Jimmie) Foxx and Ruth didn't have lengthy streaks. "DiMag" seemed to be in there every day and was getting that hit. It has stood a long time.

5

33

The Los Angeles Lakers' NBA Record Winning Streak

The Left Coast View

Mark Heisler

Around Los Angeles, the number 33 can stir up one of two memories, either the jersey number worn by Kareem Abdul-Jabbar during his tenure with the Los Angeles Lakers or the incredible winning streak by the 1971-72 Lakers. Los Angeles Times *sportswriter Mark Heisler has covered the NBA for 15 years, but hasn't witnessed a team that has even come close to that Lakers winning streak. Not even the 1995-96 Chicago Bulls who won 72 games (surpassing the Lakers old NBA record of 69 in the season of their streak). If you thought the Chicago Bulls were aging before their breakup in 1999, Heisler cited two-thirds of an aging threesome on the Lakers' front line that carried their weight in the Lakers success that season. In addition to this perspective, Heisler has also written about former Lakers coach Pat Riley in* The Lives of Riley. *Riley was also a member of that '71-72 Laker team.*

33

It wasn't the best of times or the worst of times, but it was looking like the end of times for the creaky Lakers, who in 1971 started on what I think was the greatest roll in the history of American team sports, a 33-game winning streak that lasted more than two months and included a 16-0 mark on the road, a 7-0 mark in the second game of back-to-backs, which they won by an average of 21 points and a 4-0 record in the third night of back-to-back-to-backs, which they won by an average of 12.8 points.

To the Lakers, themselves, it was even more incredible, seeing as how several, like Wilt Chamberlain and Jerry West had both been on teams that looked better, or had more expected of them. This one had tied for third in the West the year before and was eliminated by Kareem Abdul-Jabbar's Bucks in a 4-1 conference final, after which Coach Joe Mullaney was fired.

In the greater sense, this wasn't just a two-month roll. It lasted all season. The Lakers finished with 69 victories, another NBA record that stood for 24 years. In the playoffs, they rolled through the Bulls, Bucks and Knicks, 4-0, 4-2, 4-1, to an NBA championship.

Then they fell apart.

To the rest of the world...well, anything that happened in the NBA in the early 70s didn't count for too much, did it?

Years later, there would be an incredible drumroll as the Bulls advanced on the Lakers' 69 wins, but at the end of the '71-72 season, who cared that the Lakers were about to erase the 76ers' five-year-old record of 68?

If the NBA was generally accorded major league status in the early 70s, it still lagged far far behind baseball and the NFL. As late as 1980, when rookie Magic Johnson jumped center against Darryl Dawkins in the decisive game of the NBA finals, CBS carried it at 11:30 p.m. EST, on tape delay.

Eight years before? Forget the number. Something exciting in New York, like the 1970 Knicks title run, might get Madison Avenue calling it "The game of the 80s," but as soon as the home team cooled off in Gotham, the league went back into its hole. The NBA, it seemed, was Wilt scoring 100 points, in Hershey, Pa., before a handful of spectators, with 76ers publicist Harvey Pollack calling in the scores to two of the three Philadelphia newspapers.

In 1971, the *Los Angeles Times* rarely staffed Laker road games during the season, making an exception during the streak only for occasional games, and not all the big ones. On Dec. 10, when the Lakers beat the Golden State Warriors in Oakland for No. 19, pulling to within one of the Milwaukee Bucks' record, there was no one there from the *Times*.

The *Times*' Mal Florence, was there for the end of the streak, at Milwaukee on Jan. 9. However, just to show where an ordinary NBA game rated in the greater scheme of things, Sports Editor Bill Shirley brought Florence home the next day while the team continued on the road.

This, of course, flabbergasted the Lakers. Coach Bill Sharman saw Florence checking out the next day and asked where he was going.

"Bill," said Florence, "I don't cover losers."

It was a royal but fading cast that started the season. The key players, Elgin Baylor, Wilt and West were 37, 35 and 33, respectively. Their team that had been so ballyhooed three seasons before, when Chamberlain arrived from Philadelphia, had exploded spectacularly in Game 7 of the finals, when the Celtics beat them in Jack Kent Cooke's Fabulous Forum, under the balloons

Cooke had thoughtfully penned up in the rafters for the victory celebration.

Nothing very positive had happened after that, either. Coach Butch Van Breda Kolff, who had feuded with Wilt, ran off, to be replaced by Mullaney, who kowtowed to everyone, posted 46 and 48-win seasons and was fired.

Baylor had missed all but two games of the 1970-71 season after tearing an Achilles tendon.

The new coach in 1971 was Bill Sharman, an ex-Celtic of all things, coming off a stint in the American Basketball Association, with a mania for obsessive preparation and a lot of new ideas, like a "shootaround" to get the guys out of bed and thinking about that night's game.

Of course, as he later admitted, Wilt, an insomniac who liked to sleep in, wasn't an instant convert. The story goes, the first time Sharman sent someone up to Chamberlain's room to summon him to a shootaround, Wilt replied, "Tell him I'm only coming to the arena once and he can pick which one." (Both men deny the story but we include it anyway, for completeness.)

Sharman had many ideas, like running with an old team, and asking Chamberlain to concentrate on defense, rebounding and outlet passing.

Asking Wilt to change his game was like asking a mountain to move over a little bit, but Wilt said he'd try. Not that it meant much for a while. The Lakers were 6-3, when Baylor, laboring in his comeback, retired.

The next night, Friday, Nov. 5, the Lakers struggled against the Baltimore Bullets but won, 110-106, in the Forum, ending a two-game losing streak. Baylor's replacement, 23-year-old Jim McMillian, scored 22 points - he would average 18.8 that season - but no one recognized it as the beginning of an epoch.

Then the hits just started happening.

In this era, when players whine about playing back-to-back, it seems incredible that the Lakers won the first eight games in a row *in 10 days*, while playing in five different cities.

On Dec. 10, a month and five days into the streak, they beat the Phoenix Suns in the Forum for their 20th in a row, tying the Bucks' record. Two nights later, they beat the Hawks for No. 21.

Then they won another 12 in a row, the last in Atlanta, where they hammered the Hawks by 44 points.

Two days later, however, in a nationally televised Sunday game in Milwaukee, the Bucks dropped them, 120-104, led by an inspired Abdul-Jabbar, who scored 39 points and took 20 rebounds.

"It was one of those games. Everyone was so excited about it," says West, "but of all the games I ever played, I don't think I ever felt more fatigued than that game. I was so tired, it was really hard for me to play. But we did not have our normal energy. They got off to a big lead and we cut it down, but then we just did-n't have anything left. In our locker room, it was like you'd lost your mother and father, quiet, a morose feel to it."

Maybe the streak finally got too heavy for them to carry. The season ended on a better note - West's only title as a player - but then the magic slipped away.

Sharman came back the next season with an ulcer-ated larynx that permanently damaged his voice. The Lakers fell to 60 wins and were upended in the West finals by the Bulls.

Wilt retired to become coach for the ABA's San Diego Conquistadores. West retired a year later. But, for one long, shining moment, they were hell together.

The Second City View

Sam Smith

Like *Mark Heisler, Sam Smith has also covered the NBA beat for several years. Smith was on the Bulls beat for the* Chicago Tribune *in the 1995-96 season, the year the Bulls shattered the regular season record for most wins, which sparked a debatable question. What is more impressive, 33 wins in a row or 72 wins on the year? Smith, also the author of* The Jordan Rules, *helps settle the answer.*

33

Nothing, it has been said, is as good as it seems beforehand. The anticipation of a date for a dance, a new job, a good investment. The same with great sporting feats. The anticipation rarely matches the actuality.

Because what we anticipate seldom occurs.

What we least expect generally happens. Which is what made the 1995-96 Chicago Bulls basketball season, in which the team set the all-time NBA record of 72 wins as the most remarkable record in league history. Because, simply, no other record ever was expected, almost demanded, for weeks before the season ever started. There can never be a final resolution to the debate over what is the greatest record in sports. Is it DiMaggio's 56-game hitting streak, Cy Young's 511 wins, Wilt's 100 points, Ripken's consecutive games played, the Lakers' 33 straight wins? All are probably unapproachable, especially in this era of specialists, substitutions, extra rest and intense scrutiny.

Yet, not only is that when the Bulls won their 72 games to eclipse the Lakers record of 69 wins in the season they won 33 straight, the Bulls did it at a time when it was predicted before the season started. Even Jerry West, who played on that great Lakers championship team of 1971-72 and now is the general manager of the Lakers, was saying a week before the season started he believed the Bulls had a chance to break his Lakers' team's record of 69 wins in a season.

Midway through the season, after the Bulls started 41-3 and had a chance to win the three games they lost in the last minute, West's then-teammate Pat Riley was saying the Bulls had easily the most dominant team in the league and he wouldn't be surprised if they won 75 games. Which gave the Bulls the twin albatrosses for any athlete or team, pressure and expectations.

The Bulls were supposed to break a record no one had come very close to in decades. It's not how records are broken. Records happen, much like the Lakers' 33-game winning streak. That was chance and happenstance as much as anything. It, along with Wilt Chamberlain's 100 points, is probably the most unreachable record in pro basketball.

But it merely happened, and was hardly expected.

It perhaps was a few years before in 1968 when the Lakers traded for Chamberlain, thus putting together the first great threesome in NBA history of Chamberlain, Elgin Baylor and West, all considered among the top ten players in the history of the NBA.

Great things were expected. They didn't happen.

The Lakers lost in the finals two straight seasons, the second to the Knicks and the hobbling Willis Reed, and in 1971, after winning just 48 games and finishing 18 games behind the Milwaukee Bucks, the Lakers were ousted in five games in the Western Conference finals.

After Baylor retired, it was the big, aging two and Gail Goodrich. It was hardly the team to scare and dominate.

It did, to the surprise of even itself.

Jim Cleamons, who was then a rookie on that team and would later be an assistant coach on the Bulls' 72-win team, said Coach Bill Sharman was merely trying to put together a rotation with role players like Happy Hairston and Jim McMillian.

What he got was more than two months without a loss.

Keith Erickson, a seldom used reserve on that '71-72 team, said the retirement of Baylor was actually a blessing since it opened up playing time for more players and allowed a more diversified offense.

That all said, it still was highly unexpected and without much pressure.

It was a big national story, Cleamons remembers, *Sports Illustrated* covers and all that, but the NBA was hardly big news back then. Before the Bucks 20-game winning streak the season before, the previous record was 18 straight by the Knicks, and Cleamons said when the Lakers passed these marks, the pressure eased dramatically.

They just kept playing and winning and seeing how far they could take it. It would end after 33 straight, just beyond two months without a loss, a joyous ride that established Lakers' dominance that season with a record 12.3 per game victory margin and a relatively easy five-game NBA Finals win over the Knicks.

And the conditions weren't what they are today: No charter jets, no first class hotel accommodations, some weeks with games on three straight nights and, as Hairston would later point out, "They didn't have the Clippers, Timberwolves and Kings to beat up on."

Though the Lakers would have their share of patsies. It was true that by the 90s rivalries had disappeared in the NBA with the many expansions so that Eastern and Western teams played one another just twice. The Lakers were playing their opponents five and six times a season then, and there had been a radical expansion movement in 1970 that created division play for the first time. Buffalo, Cleveland and Portland were added to the league.

It has been pointed out by many that when the Bulls won 72 games in '95-96, it was in an already expansion-diluted league that took on four new teams in the late 1980s, and another two, Toronto and Vancouver, in 1995. Plus, players now traveled in unheard of style with charter aircraft stocked with Roman feasts, never playing more than two straight games and most teams having their own practice facilities and more trainers and masseuses than Sharman's team had assistant coaches.

The life of a 90s NBA player was far easier than a 70s NBA player, but vastly more complicated.

Especially with arguably the greatest and certainly the most publicized player ever in Michael Jordan and the more infamous player in Dennis Rodman.

It was when Rodman was traded to the Bulls just before the start of the '95-96 season started that talk of 70 wins began almost immediately.

Jordan had returned from his baseball retirement to international headlines late the previous season, but his conditioning wasn't good enough, and the Bulls weren't strong enough at power forward. They needed someone to fetch the ball, as Coach Phil Jackson liked to say. So they gambled on Rodman, who led the league in rebounding average the last four seasons, and in suspensions. He was MTV on pills, tattooed, pierced and multi-hued. There weren't enough knobs on your color TV to fix what he had. He was the most controversial player in the league. But he could fetch that ball like no one else.

And he was paired with the most spectacular, most famous and most photographed athlete of all time, Jordan. There were instant nicknames, like Superman, Batman and Robin.

The marketing had begun before the games. Now all they had to do was fill in the blank at least 70 times.

Jordan spent the summer working out as never before, and the Bulls had the "Big Three" of basketball, a trio to match Larry Bird, Kevin McHale and Robert Parish as well as Chamberlain, West and Baylor. Plus, Jordan and Scottie Pippen had been on three championship teams each, Rodman two. They all knew how to win.

And it's all they did.

Even when the Lakers won 69, they finished 30-7, good but not the stuff of superlatives. The Bulls never had a down period. After the 41-3 start they lost two straight games on a road trip in the Rocky Mountain time zone, first after they had come back from 31 down to actually lead before losing. That ended an 18-game winning streak, their best. In the next two months, they had three six-game winning streaks and a seven with just four individual losses mixed in. Everyone knew what they were going for, yet no one could stop them. Their opponents were led by MVP players, Hakeem Olajuwon, David Robinson, Charles Barkley and future star Shaquille O'Neal. All were voted among the top 50 players in NBA history by then and they were just more fodder.

To beat the Bulls once that season was to make a team's season. Everyone wanted to deny them immortality. It was the ultimate boast. The Bulls told everyone they could do it, then went out and did it with everyone watching. It's not boasting if you can. The Bulls dominated that season like only perhaps the Lakers of '71-72. They won by an average of 12.2 per game and finished a streak of 44 straight wins at home.

The media contingent with the Bulls on a daily basis, Cleamons said, was greater than the Lakers had for the finals in 1972. It was, at times, more circus than sport, more thrill show than skill show. Rodman would be suspended for attacking a referee during the season, causing the media horde to grow, the demands to become even more extreme.

Yet, the Bulls would continue to win, game after game, dominating even the best teams, averaging wins by more than points in games against teams that defeated them in previous games.

By the time the Bulls were going for their 70th win, it was madness. Helicopters followed the team bus from the practice facility in Deerfield, Ill., to Milwaukee. It was the most media ever at a Bucks game.

Everyone came every night to see if the Bulls would lose, to the see if the Bulls could break the quarter-century old record, and it's just what the Bulls did. When the spotlight is brightest, the pressure is most intense.

The Bulls and the nation put 70 out there as a goal and dared the Bulls to reach it. And reminded them for seven months about it. Asked them everywhere they went, before and after every game, when they were tired or happy, at the All-Star game and over Christmas dinner at home. Could they do it? Would they do it? It would be a failure, in effect, not to do it.

No one ever had been asked to do that, not DiMaggio, not Ripken, not Chamberlain. Those records just happened. The Bulls' record was a dare, which made it that much more precious and all the more rare.

6

88

The UCLA Bruins' Record College Basketball Winning Streak

The Center's View
Bill Walton

During *Bill Walton's era at UCLA, the Walton Gang put together a winning streak of 88 straight games that marked the peak of Coach John Wooden's career at UCLA. They won seven straight NCAA championships, another number that may never be matched in college basketball. Two of those teams were the undefeated editions of '71-'72 and '72-'73, the only back-to-back undefeated championship teams in the Wooden era. Overall, UCLA won ten NCAA titles in a 12-year span from 1964 to 1975. After also excelling in the NBA, Walton was elected to the Basketball Hall of Fame. Since Walton experienced the rigors of playing night-in, night-out on the professional level, he differed in opinion with the L.A.Times' Mark Heisler, who as you read earlier, labeled the Lakers' 33-game winning streak as "...the greatest roll in American team sports."*

88

The college game is completely different from the NBA. The pro game is designed for the best team to win. The length of the games and seasons, the officials, the rules and the speed of the game enables the best team to win on a regular basis. That's why you very rarely have upsets at the championship level. Collegiately, the rules are such that even the severest underdogs have a real chance at winning.

How interesting that both the Lakers' and the Bruins' streaks were going on at the same time in the same city. Not to take anything away from the Lakers' accomplishment because they were truly phenomenal, but it was all done in the course of two months. The UCLA streak covered 2 1/2 years without a loss.

That's something we're very proud of in one sense, but find disappointing and frustrating in the bigger picture. We had an unbelievably great college basketball team. For us to have lost at all was embarrassing. Coach Wooden taught us to be the best; and to think, act, and expect to be the champions. When we lost those games at the end of our senior year, it was truly devastating. It changed our lives forever.

If we had won 105 straight, as we should have, then we could sit back today and say, "Yeah, we really did something."

As it is, having lost to Notre Dame on January 19, 1974, ending the streak, we can only sit back and say to ourselves, "Well, what if...?" That's a tough way to go through life.

Coach Wooden told us every day, from the very beginning until graduation four years later, "Guys. Do your best, but don't ever beat yourself. When you beat yourself, it's the worst kind of defeat that you'll ever suffer. You'll never get over it."

We thought he was nuts. About that and all the other stuff he used to tell us. About how to tie your shoes and put your socks on; how to tuck your shirts in, and about being quick, without hurrying, never mistaking activity for achievement; failing to prepare is preparing to fail; it's not how big you are, it's how big you play, it's not how high you jump, it's where you are and when you jump; basketball is not a game of size and strength, it's a game of skill, timing, and position. All the maims that rolled off of Wooden's tongue like poetry seemed so out of place when we were dominating.

We thought all that stuff was just ludicrous, then it all started crumbling. As I sit here today twenty-five years after playing for the great Coach Wooden, our house is a shrine to UCLA basketball, full of the pyramids, pictures of the coach and all his books. He was such a great teacher, such an inspiration. I'm just sad and embarrassed that I'm such a slow learner.

In our family, because of the role that Digger Phelps and Notre Dame has had in ruining my life, it's always been tough whenever anybody brings up the Fightin' Irish. As a young father, raising four boys, when I had to discipline them, lay down the law or be the bad guy who had to say no, my kids would get very agitated and very frustrated. They'd look at me with a scowl on their face and say, "Dad I'm going to Notre Dame."

I was flabbergasted, crestfallen because my life is the result of the greatness of UCLA and John Wooden. When you're touched by something really special, your life is never the same again. Ever since I've been with John Wooden, I've been constantly searching to try to duplicate that environment.

As previously noted, I'm a slow learner. I've since come to learn that Notre Dame is an outstanding school. I just wish they hadn't ruined my life back then, January 19, 1974, one of the bleakest days of my life.

We had a 12-point lead and the ball with a couple minutes left in the game and we gave it away. We could not finish them off. It was so sad. It's one thing to play and get beat, but when you beat yourself... Wooden was right - you never get over it. I can still see the closing moments of that game. I can still see the band going crazy. I can still see the student body at Notre Dame charging the court. I can see them carrying Digger Phelps off. A recurring nightmare that just won't go away.

We never really talked about the streak while it was going on. We knew we were the best team. We knew we could and should win every single game. We were favorites from the beginning. We were expected to win. The surprise came from losing.

Knowing full well that you can never go back and knowing that it's not good for your mental health to look back, still I sure wish I could have the last couple of months of my senior year all over again. I had suffered a crippling injury two weeks before the Notre Dame game on January 19. I had been low-bridged by some guard who came in and undercut my legs. I landed on my back and cracked a couple of bones in my spine and had been unable to play for the previous two weeks prior to the Notre Dame game. The Notre Dame game was the first time I had played basketball in two weeks and I had to wear a corset with some steel rods inserted into it for some support.

We had such a great team with so much talent. The interesting thing was that our senior season, the year that we lost, it was the squad that had the most talent. While talent is part of the equation, much more important is team chemistry, the right spirit and the right attitude.

The first year of our varsity career at UCLA in 1972, we set the NCAA record for the largest winning margin in the history of college basketball, well in excess of 30-plus points per game. In that season, teams tried very hard to beat us by playing basketball, by trying to outrun us, by trying to outshoot us. They had absolutely no chance.

The next year, our junior year, opponents had come to the conclusion that winning was out of the question so they wanted to keep the scores down. They would just stall and not shoot at all. Even though we were playing good basketball, the air had been taken out of the ball and the game, so the length of the competition was very short. We could not accomplish our personal goals of playing great and racing up and down the court, celebrating the greatness of life and UCLA. That trend continued through our junior and senior year, so statistically the numbers just weren't there.

In spite of all this, we were constantly improving. That was one of the strengths of John Wooden. He took players and people and made them better over the course of our years with him. Coach Wooden was not so much a coach as he was a teacher. His only goal in life has always been to make other people's lives better. He has succeeded magnificently in that. All of us have gone on to enjoy fabulous lives because of the lessons we learned from our hero, our teacher, Coach Wooden.

Playing for UCLA was equal parts, privilege and joy. It was so special to be a part of that team and that era. We all have such fond memories. Our team has stayed incredibly close over the years. We're constantly having reunions and unique events. We're all close personal friends. Most of us still live in the Southern California area. It's great to be able to sit back and laugh and joke with all the guys on the team about how much fun we had and how none of the guys were ever willing to pass me the ball.

There was nothing like being a UCLA Bruin playing for John Wooden. UCLA gave me the greatest gifts that anyone could ever give. They taught me how to learn, how to think; they taught me that the ultimate winners are the ones that build on a foundation to enable you to get to the top realizing that ultimately the quickest thinkers, the sharpest decision makers will be the biggest and most consistent winners. It was truly the greatest time of my life.

The Heir's View
Kent Benson

When *UCLA's 88-game winning streak was stopped by Notre Dame in January, 1974, Kent Benson was playing down the road in Bloomington where he was Indiana University's leading rebounder in the first of his four years with the Hoosiers. In 1975, Benson's sophomore year, the Hoosiers finished the regular season undefeated, but lost to the University of Kentucky in the Mideast regional final and finished the year at 31-1. UCLA eventually beat Kentucky in the national championship game for its final NCAA title under Coach John Wooden. A year later, the Hoosiers won the NCAA title with an undefeated season, 32-0, the last undefeated Division I team through 1998-99. In his junior year as the Hoosiers center, Benson was voted the Final Four MVP in '76. As a member of those outstanding Hoosier teams, Benson was familiar with what it took to put together extended winning streaks.*

88

I loved the game of basketball, but my involvement in being a farm boy kept me pretty busy. I had opportunities to play, but never really sat down to watch much basketball. When I went to IU, I became very familiar with Big Ten basketball and the All-Americans. These days, I'm a fan of my daughters. I've got four daughters and they play basketball. Of course, they take precedence over Indiana basketball and, for that matter, any other basketball. But I am a fan of the Indiana Hoosiers and that's where it stops.

Being born and raised in Indiana, I was always aware of the Hoosiers. I must say that, being raised Roman Catholic, Notre Dame was kind of put on a pedestal, so Notre Dame was probably up there at number one. Number two would have been Purdue because of my agricultural background and then Indiana because a lot of people in our community were staunch Indiana basketball fans.

The main reason for our success was Coach (Bob) Knight's recruiting, his ability to put together talent and character to create such team unity. We were very close on the court. Off the court, we did our own things. When it came time to practice or to play, we were very focused.

In '75, we had Steve Green and John Laskowski. They were probably the most noted of that team. Of course—Quinn Buckner, Scott May, Tom Abernethy, Bobby Wilkerson, Jim Crews—not to leave any of my teammates out, but when you're able to put together a group of individuals who were as talented as those individuals, with a willingness to come together and do the things Coach wanted done, I think that was one of the biggest reasons for the success. We were winners. We knew what it took to win and we were willing to do what it took to win. That was to improve ourselves in the off-season individually, then collectively when we came back together during the first part of the school year.

UCLA's seven national consecutive championships, then 88 consecutive wins are pretty awesome records in any book. I don't think you could say one (record) is any better than the other because they're both incredible. When you look at 88 consecutive wins, that's pretty phenomenal in itself and I think that's going to be a record that will stand the test of time.

I was a freshman in 1974 when that record was broken. I didn't watch so much what other people were doing as much as what we were doing. Character and attitude would be the ingredients for a winning streak. I'll always say this: Successful people do the things that unsuccessful people don't and won't do.

All the players I mentioned had the character and attitude I'm talking about, both on the court and off the court. You can also mix in leadership abilities. Steve Green and John Laskowski provided more than the "rah rah" type of leadership. They talked to you, they helped you improve your game. They rose above mediocrity and I think that's indicative of every one of these players.

Quinn Buckner was a leader when he first stepped on the court at Indiana. When Quinn was on the court, it was like having Coach Knight on the court. Quinn did a great job of being a leader in many aspects of the game. He understood the game and what needed to be accomplished.

I really believe Coach Knight knew when he recruited the type of individuals it took to mold a team like that together. He did a tremendous amount of homework to put together a team with players he felt were coachable. I think that's the key to the success of any team.

There were times when he was really hard on me. Know what? Had he let me slide, I would never have been able to play 11 years in the NBA. He knew what it took to motivate each individual.

There isn't a day that goes by that people aren't bringing up the '75 and '76 team, especially the undefeated national championship team. For me, it's like it happened just yesterday because I've been living it every day in conversations with people. I don't mind that. I'm very honored that people want to talk about it and still remember us after all these years.

I could only speak for ourselves and what we experienced and I'm sure that the UCLA players who were part of their success feel the same way.

7

47

The Oklahoma Sooners' Record College Football Winning Streak

The Booth View
Chris Schenkel

Oklahoma's *47-game winning streak began in 1953 and ended in 1957 under Coach Bud Wilkinson. As an ABC-TV play-by-play man in college football, Chris Schenkel worked side by side with Wilkinson in the broadcast booth and developed a unique perspective. Not only did Schenkel personally witness why Wilkinson was successful, but called the games for the best college football programs week after week.*

47

I was in New York City broadcasting the New York Giants football games and I was also doing a nightly sports show there, so I followed not only pro football, but college football. I didn't start broadcasting college football until 1966 along with Bud Wilkinson. The Giants' head coach was Steve Owen, also from Oklahoma, so he talked a lot about Bud's ability and winning streak. It was on the lips of anybody who loved college football.

It made great copy, not only for radio and television sportscasts, but also for newspapers, whether they were dailies, weeklies or whatever. Everything was so positive about the streak and, of course, everybody that played Oklahoma was looking to knock them off.

I always had fun talking with Bud on the 47-game winning streak because one of the Giants' defensive backs was a boy named Dick Lynch from Notre Dame. He was the one who scored the touchdown that broke the streak, so I used to kid Bud. I'd get him riled up a little bit by saying, "Dick Lynch said 'hello,' Bud." Dick was really one of our most outstanding defensive halfbacks on the Giants.

I've been on all sides of it, I guess. When it first happened, I was truly amazed, flabbergasted and astounded. But, later when I got to know and work with Bud Wilkinson, the architect of that long winning streak, I knew why it happened. He was the epitome of what a leader and a college coach should be.

Bud probably had the best demeanor when it came to recruiting. I found out after having met a lot of the players, they would tell me how he came to their parents' home and how he treated them. There was no phony baloney, everything on the top of the table. He was concerned with what their child, their son, was going to do with higher education along with playing football for him. He apparently made a lot of promises, none of which were ever broken.

That was one of the big qualities. I've bumped into so many coaches and I know about different recruiting methods and recruiting types - the hard-hitters, the hammers - but Bud Wilkinson was the true gentleman. He always was, I think, from the moment he was born in Minnesota. He was one of a kind. That, in a nutshell, would tell you why those Oklahoma teams were so great.

I got to know a lot of the players like Darrell Royal and his wife Edith, two of my best friends. I learned about Bud's qualities and how everyone looked up to him on the team, whether a player was on the third string or first string. It's not surprising that his team would play as a unit - almost like a family - and go undefeated because Bud recruited the right type of young men. Men who were going to make it through college, get their degree, yet also use their God-given athletic abilities.

It'd be sort of difficult to describe the mannerisms unless you knew Bud. You'd have to have spent hours after hours with Bud Wilkinson to really have a definition for "mannerisms." I say this because, at his retirement party sometime before his much too early death, my spotter who had been with us through all the years gave me a statistic. As I got up to talk about Bud in Oklahoma City, I said, "Bud, I have a statistic for you, and I know neither one of us likes statistics, but this is one that you wouldn't even believe."

So I waited a moment. Then I said, "Bud, you did more television games with me than you coached!"

Of course, he was flabbergasted because he coached a helluva lot of games, but we did a lot of telecasts together, too.

He was impeccable in his preparation for the telecasts and getting knowledge of the offenses and defenses for both teams, and he learned television. He had a very good start.

There was *The Bud Wilkinson Show* while he was at Oklahoma, so he learned some of the techniques about television. But he learned a lot more when he started broadcasting football. Like the great student he was, he was a student of television. He couldn't understand a lot of things, like why television did things this way or that way, because he thought it was foolish. And I think most times he was right.

You could always count on him never to let you down. Never to, in a menacing sort of fashion, correct you on the air. He might slip you a note and say, "Chris, you missed the tackle on the last play." Nowadays, the expert commentators and the play-by-play guys like to nail the other person. But not Bud Wilkinson.

He ruled with an iron fist, but had a velvet glove on. He was somebody who could get across his point because he had the intelligence to do it. He probably knew the lyrics to more Hawaiian songs than any mainlander because it happened to be one of his hobbies. Can you name a Hawaiian song? He'd sing it for you. I could go through the dictionary and come up with all the positive words and it would fit Bud. You could start with "able," or start with "adroit," but I'd say most of all he was considerate of his fellow human beings regardless of their age. Especially young men.

He had two sons of his own who were great athletes. One is among the country's foremost eye surgeons and the other was an All-American quarterback at Duke. He treated his OU Sooners just like he wanted his sons to be treated.

Now there's so much competition. Almost every team is extremely good because the athletes are. I don't know why, but they're bigger. Is it from vitamins or what? They play a different brand of football. I'm not sure teams could ever get to 47, and I'm enough of a historian, a nostalgic person, that I hope they never do. Let me put it this way. I haven't met a coach yet that can equal him as a football expert and a person, so maybe that'll give you a better idea why I don't ever want it broken. It's a phenomenal achievement.

Nebraska. Oklahoma. Southern Cal. Notre Dame. There are just so many great programs, but I still don't think they'll reach 47 in a row unless they play "Podunk" every week.

A lot of people ask me about the biggest thrills in my long career. Of course, there's broadcasting the Olympic games and so many other things, but living through the 47-victory streak with Bud Wilkinson coaching was a thrill. The thrill is highlighted by having known this man and calling him my best friend.

The Coach's View

Darrell Royal

ormer University of Texas Coach Darrell Royal knows something about winning streaks. After dropping the 1948 season opener against Santa Clara, Royal and the Sooners won 21 in a row in Royal's junior and senior years. His senior season, a perfect 11-0, was capped by a 35-0 Sugar Bowl win over LSU. After Royal graduated, the Sooners won their first ten games of the 1950 season before losing the Sugar Bowl against Kentucky to end the 31-game winning streak. In Royal's first year as head coach at the University of Texas in 1957, Oklahoma had won 41 in a row before meeting the Longhorns Oct. 12. Though the Sooners won that game and five more before losing to Notre Dame, 7-0, on Nov. 16, the Longhorns finished 6-3-1 to reverse a 1-9 season the year before. From Oct. 5, 1968, to Dec. 5, 1970, Coach Royal directed the Longhorns to 30 wins in a row. His perspective of OU's 47-game winning streak starts with his reflections on his own collegiate days with the Sooners.

47

We had good football players. He had assembled a bunch of outstanding players who started with Coach (Jim) Tatum. Coach Jim Tatum was there in 1946. Coach Wilkinson became head coach in '47 and molded the group. He was an excellent teacher. He taught his subject well. There was no confusion in the players' minds as to what they were supposed to do. They were clear on what their assignments were and why their assignments were given to them, clear on how the team functioned and how their assignments fit in with the rest of the team and their teammates. Because there was no confusion among the players, they could go full speed and be aggressive.

If a player is confused to me on film, he looks like a guy who is timid. You can't tell sometimes whether a player is timid or whether he just doesn't know what to do. Coach Wilkinson took all the confusion out. It was very simple. Players were informed when they went into the game.

Coach Wilkinson's theory on offense was that in a ten-yard span, you try to make three-and-a-third yards a play that results in a first down. You move the chains, then you try to make another first down. Every now and then, there was a long run that took place in there. There was sometimes a pass play that made more than the average, but basically we were just trying to make first downs. That's the way runners ran and the way the play-calling was done. If you made a succession of first downs, you got into the end zone.

I tried to do a lot of things that he did, but I made

sure that I didn't even attempt to have his personality. Everybody has to use his own personality, his own approach and work things his own way, but I used his ideas of making first downs and using field position. We were always more run-oriented. I had the reputation of being anti-pass, but in the big ballgames we won and we won by throwing.

Playing quarterback under him was a real privilege because it taught me a style and an approach to offensive football that I used until the last day I coached. They say, "Well, every play is designed for a touchdown." That's the biggest bunch of crap that ever came down the pike.

We had a real heavy graduation and I thought what the '50 team accomplished was really outstanding. The quarterback was Claude Arnold. I always thought he did more with that '50 team than any quarterback who had played at Oklahoma. There were some great sophomores who came along. Billy Vessels (the '52 Heisman Trophy winner) was among that group. Buck McPhail and Max Boydston. They won the next ten, then lost to Kentucky and Babe Parilli in the Sugar Bowl.

I followed them with a lot of interest, of course. I went back a number of years, right after I got out. I'd go back in the spring when they had a varsity-alumni game. I played in that thing for several years, actually, while I was coaching. I'd go back to Norman, work out two or three days, then play.

My first coaching job was at North Carolina State. I was coaching on the freshman team and was lucky enough to have a guy like Beatty Feathers who let a guy coach. He didn't give me a lot of instructions - he gave me free rein. It was a great experience learning under Coach Feathers. I was there a year, then went to the University of Tulsa as the varsity backfield coach. Again, lucky enough to coach under Buddy Brothers who let me coach the offensive backs the way I wanted to. He never gave me any instructions or corrected me in any shape, form or fashion. He seemed to have confidence in turning me loose.

The next year, I went to Mississippi State as an assistant coach. I was coaching the backfield again for Murray Warmath and he did the same thing. I was able to coach from the day I first started and not be under the supervision of someone older and more experienced. They just let me go ahead with my mistakes and I learned as I went. After three years, I became a head coach in the Canadian professional league (1953). I coached the Edmonton Eskimos one year, then left and went back to Mississippi State as head coach.

I think I learned more coaching in Canada than I did in any other single year. It was my first head coaching job. I had to deal with the Board of Directors. I had to deal with the media every day. The local paper would come and talk to me after every practice and, certainly, after every game. I showed the film to a local support group. I think they called it the "Quarterback Club."

All of that experience and I had full control. I was the head coach at only 27 years old. I had to do a hard-selling job to those guys who played professional football. I was just barely out of college and had never played professional football. Talking to the squad, trying handle the morale and trying to handle, in some form, discipline, yet knowing that they are professionals. You can't coach them exactly like you coach a college team, so it was a great learning experience. I had to do a pretty intense selling job on those guys to get them to believe in what I was trying to teach and what we were trying to do. I think I did that by the end of the season.

I would see Coach Wilkinson at coaching conventions. Then in 1957, I remember the game against Oklahoma, but I never thought during the course of that game that Coach Wilkinson was on the other side of the field. I was intent on our team and what our team was doing. Of course, we met and visited with each other before the kickoff and we always met after the ballgames just briefly. Shook hands, then parted and went our own ways. I never was aware that any other coach was on the other side of the field. I don't ever recall looking across at an opposing coach.

We extended them that day. We played a decent ballgame. It was 21-7.

Any time you put a winning streak together, you've got some games in there when you think the game is gone and then, suddenly, something happens and you win.

We were playing UCLA (1970) and we were at 20-something during that time (actually 22). We had the ball, third-and-about 15, and there were 19 seconds left in the game. We were at about midfield. You can't have much hope of winning that ballgame, but our quarterback threw a touchdown pass to a split receiver. We won the ballgame (20-17)! People were leaving the stands and they heard all this roaring and hollering. They wondered what happened. They were going to their cars, piling out of there and they just couldn't believe that the hollering was for a touchdown. Any time you have a long winning streak, there are some games like that.

We had a game where we had to come from behind against Arkansas, 14-0, going into the fourth quarter (Dec. 6, 1969: Texas won, 15-14). That's one thing about winning streaks. You've got to have a little luck somewhere in there because you just don't get ahead of everyone and stay ahead all the time. It's just impossible. In '63, an undefeated season, we were behind and we put in a reserve quarterback, who was a better passer and he led us down the field. We scored right at the end of the game to beat Texas A&M (15-13).

Coach Wilkinson's 47-game winning streak was unbelievable. To think he had two winning streaks, one of 31 and one of 47. That's unbelievable. Our 30-game winning streak at Texas has lasted through the years. No one has broken that recently. I just don't see how anyone can match 47.

8

2,632

Cal Ripken's Record For Consecutive Games Played

The Press Box View

Ken Rosenthal

or the record, let it be known that Baltimore Sun
writer Ken Rosenthal wasn't always on the same
page with Cal Ripken, Jr. on how far The Streak
*should have gone. It was reflected by one incident in
1998 when a foul ball off the bat of Ripken took out
Rosenthal's lap top computer while he was working in
the press box. Needless to say, the computer hardly
measured up to the durability of Ripken. Nevertheless,
agree or disagree, Rosenthal's objectivity was unaf-
fected as expressed in his view of The Streak.*

2,632

Mark down the number - 2,632. No one will ever play that many consecutive games again. No one will even try. Lou Gehrig's monument at Yankee Stadium says his "amazing record of 2,130 consecutive games should stand for all time." Cal Ripken reduced forever to 54 years. And he turned 16 years into forever.

The number 2,632 will be frozen in history, as eternal as 56 (the length of Joe DiMaggio's hitting streak) and 511 (Cy Young's career victory total).

The Streak began as a simple reflection of Ripken's desire to play and help the Baltimore Orioles win. It evolved into a saving grace for his sport and an object lesson for his nation. Ultimately, it grew bigger than the man, bigger than his team, bigger than the game - so big, that it not only made history, but also sparked controversy.

Critics suggested that Ripken sit down whenever he wasn't hitting. The debate grew more intense as he played through a debilitating back injury in the second half of '97 and a sub-par campaign in '98.

His decision to sit on Sept. 20, in '98, came one month after his 38th birthday and more than three years after breaking Gehrig's record. Ripken finally decided that it was in his best interests and the Orioles' best interests to move on.

"Baseball has always been a team game, and I've always thought the focus should be on the team," Ripken said. "There have been times during the streak when the focus was on the streak and I never felt totally comfortable about that. It was time to change the subject and restore the focus back to where it should be."

The Streak began when the Orioles played at Memorial Stadium, before the rise of all-sports radio, all-sports television and the Internet. It spanned five presidential terms. It survived three Orioles owners, eight managers and countless aches and pains. It started early in the Me Decade and lasted almost until the end of the millennium.

A century from now, few will recall the paradox of The Streak, how it combined elements of selfishness and unselfishness. Few will even remember that he would have been a Hall of Famer based on his playing achievements alone.

The Streak was Ripken. Ripken was The Streak.

What people will remember is the physical stamina, mental strength and the incredible fortune that it took for one man to play so many consecutive games. What people will remember is September 6, 1995. The night Ripken broke Gehrig's record at Camden Yards will endure as one of the most special moments in sports history.

How special was it?

It left even ESPN motormouth Chris Berman speechless. Berman remained silent for more than 20 minutes as an emotional Ripken took several curtain calls, then a victory lap around Camden Yards. The video images included President Clinton shaking his fists in exultation, and Ripken's tough-guy father, Cal Sr., fighting back tears.

What could anyone possibly say?

Ripken's night helped dash the cynicism that surrounded the national pastime after a strike disrupted the 1994 and '95 seasons. The Great Home Run Derby of '98 had a similar impact, completing the recovery that Ripken started. But that was a series of moments, not just one.

Ripken's night was different. Ripken's night was singular. Ripken's night touched us all. Iron Man, Family Man, Man of the People - Ripken was all of those things that night, just as he'd been virtually his entire career.

Joe DiMaggio was there, watching with another Hall of Famer, Frank Robinson. DiMaggio had been Gehrig's teammate. He, too, was emotional. Ripken did not intend to set the record, at least not at first. His pursuit just sort of evolved, day after day, season after season, until Gehrig's 2,130 came within reach.

The Streak was his destiny. The Streak is his legacy. Was it more a triumph of will than skill? No, Ripken had to be good enough to merit his place in the lineup every day. Was it more about individual goals than team goals? No, Ripken's managers and teammates always wanted him to play, believing he gave them the best chance to win.

Perhaps Ripken's career numbers would be better if he had taken the occasional day off. But no one knows that for sure, and how much better could his numbers be, anyway? He is a .276 lifetime hitter. He hit a major-league record 345 homers as a shortstop before moving to third base. He also holds 12 fielding records.

Like Ripken, The Streak was complex, not easily categorized. Ripken never imagined such a positive endeavor creating negative fallout. Playing every day, was to quote the title of his autobiography, "The Only Way I Know."

If only it were that simple.

Some believed The Streak created an environment in which one player was more important than the team, disrupting the natural order of a major league clubhouse. Ripken received special privileges, staying in hotels separate from the team, setting his own work schedules before games, enjoying the equivalent of valet service at Camden Yards. It isn't unusual for teams to allow double standards for superstars. But Ripken's privileges extended to his friend, Brady Anderson, a lesser player. Some teammates grew resentful. How much did it hurt the club?

Well, the Orioles reached the American League Championship Series in both 1996 and '97, and it certainly wasn't Ripken's fault that they didn't advance further. But in recent years, they have been perceived as a selfish team.

Former manager Davey Johnson antagonized the Ripken clique when he moved the All-Star shortstop to third base in 1996. Manny Alexander, the player who initially took over at short, said Ripken barely talked to him during that time. The Streak was a secondary concern then - Johnson wanted to assert his authority, seize control of the clubhouse. But in 1998, with Ray Miller as manager, the issue became unavoidable.

Ripken's quest seemed pointless, even damaging. Third-base prospect Willis Otanez broke his wrist when the Orioles tried him in right field, protecting The Streak. Another third-base prospect, Ryan Minor, started at first base rather than his natural position.

Ripken could not directly control his organization's decisions or his teammates' jealousies. He could control his playing time, or so it was thought. It might be more accurate to say that his playing time came to control him. He was afraid of the unknown - a day off was the one thing for which this preparation freak couldn't prepare. But ultimately, Ripken knew that if he didn't act, the team might act for him. Ending The Streak on the Orioles' final home game of '98 gave him the entire winter to formulate a new approach.

It wasn't as if he retired - Ripken began the '99 season as the Orioles' starting third baseman, though Miller planned to sit him 10 to 15 games. But it was time, especially with Ripken's skills starting to decline.

He brought honor to his team, his sport, his city. He became a role model for millions. And somewhere along the line, a boy's simple desire to play evolved into a man's stubborn desire to protect what he had.

That made Ripken human and, in a sense, even more remarkable. How could a mere mortal have kept going for so long?

The Ump's View
Steve Palermo

When Cal Ripken, Jr. took himself out of a game after his incredible streak of 2,632 consecutive games played, he did so thoughtfully and voluntarily. Steve Palermo took himself out of Major League Baseball on impulse. On July 6, 1991, Palermo also acted voluntarily, but with barely a moment to think, when he ran to the aid of two waitresses who were being robbed and beaten in the parking lot of a Dallas restaurant. As a result, Palermo took a bullet in his back. The game earlier in the night between the Texas Rangers and the California Angels was the last one Palermo worked as an American League umpire. From someone who enthusiastically made the calls the moment he stepped on a major league diamond in 1978, Palermo offers his perspective on a player who, with the same vigor, took the field for every single game between May 30, 1982, and Sept. 20, 1998.

2,632

To look at somebody who walked into the league in 1982 and played baseball each and every day until 1998, you can't help but see it's a phenomenal streak. Just to be in the league for that long is quite an accomplishment. I think the amazing thing to me is that having played a position where there are so many injuries, so much physicality, he was able to accomplish this. It's really beyond belief.

With umpiring, you're out there all nine innings. In reality, if you look at it from an umpiring standpoint, players only played four-and-a-half innings because they sat down for four-and-half, though there's time they spend at bat, and they're out on the field for four-and-half. If you have a streak that goes as long as Cal Ripken's which went for 16 years, I suppose an ump's would be considered 32 years because an ump has been out there twice as long.

The thing that impresses you most of all is that we, as umpires, jump from position to position. With Cal, he's playing the same position. Umpires are going to see different things every single day that are going to pique your interest. You're at home plate one day, so you're very, very alert. You're very much into the game. Not to say that you're not at third, second and first, but there are different responsibilities and different duties. With a guy like Cal, he showed up and played shortstop every single day. To some, that might seem boring. To Cal, it seemed like he asked himself, "What am I going to do today? What new thing am I going to experience today out on the baseball field?"

In 1982, I saw Cal Ripken break in. I was in

Baltimore when he came in and played in his first
game. He was over at third base, then Earl Weaver had
the idea to move him over to shortstop. He thought
that he could be a stopgap. He knew Cal was a big kid,
might not have been all that rangy, but what he lacked
in that half-step to three-quarters-of-a-step to get to a
ball he made up with intelligence. I think you're going
to get to more balls by intelligence than you will by
your athletic abilities because at some point athletic
abilities will diminish. At the same time, you're never
going to lose your intelligence. If anything, it's going to
get sharper as time goes on. That's exactly what happened with Cal Ripken.

He had a nice presence about him. He came in
not walking around like he knew it all. The thing that
impressed me more than anything else was that he
asked all the right questions. It wasn't an obligatory
question, but a question to try and learn. It seemed
like he was always asking a very pertinent question to
a situation. That's what strikes you about him being a
real leader, if not by way of voice, you knew it was by
way of action. He knew the right things to do, whom
to hit as far as the cutoff man and where to be when
you get a relay throw from the outfield. He just knew
the proper positions to be in. He knew he needed to
back up a second baseman in case there was an over-
throw. I talked with him through the course of a game
in between innings and he would dissect plays. He
brought up situations from the inning before and it was
always the question of, "What if...?" What if this would
have happened instead of what actually took place?

He was always thinking. He was one step ahead
so that he had a good idea, "Should we run into this
play again, I know what I'm supposed to do. I know
what I should be doing. I know what position I should
be in if this play takes place."

When we would come into Kansas City, take a
look at a guy like George Brett. In Milwaukee, a guy
like Robin Yount. We knew they were playing and, if

they weren't, it's not that they were sitting on the bench. It's that they were on the disabled list. You really marvel at some of these athletes who, each and every day, put forth their best. When the bell rang, they knew that they were going to be there. They were consistent. They were in the lineup. Can you imagine being a manager, after 16 years, and either in the fourth, or fifth or sixth place in the lineup, putting the name "Ripken" in? Then you build a lineup around him. Every single day, for 16 years, you're putting that name somewhere in the middle of the lineup.

Generally, you don't have a young guy come in and play consistently for 162 games. With Ripken, he was in there every single day. A manager like Earl Weaver and each and every manager who succeeded Weaver, knew they could count on him every day out in the field. So it made it easier that they could count on him being in the lineup. It became an automatic thing after awhile and we took it for granted after Ripken's third or fourth year. Then he started to rip off time and go into five, six and seven years. Now, you're saying, "This is a heckuva streak. What's going on?" Then for 14 years, 15 years, 16 years?

If you took a poll around the nation of people who showed up every single day for 16 years, you wouldn't have many names. The percentage would be minimal at best. Most jobs that we have in this country don't require all the travel, all the work and all the pounding your body would take out on the baseball field. Cal is one of the most durable, but when you take a look at him you understand why he was able to do what he did. He is very well-prepared.

For the longest time in the American League when I was there, he was considered to be one of the strongest, if not the strongest guy. We had a lot of strong guys in the league at the time. Big guys. You're talking about Jim Rice, Don Baylor and you could go on and on. Big, strong, sturdy, rock hard guys and this guy (Ripken) was there every day. As strong as he was, he was very limber. To watch him around shortstop and make the plays he did, I could just remember Cal's patented plays. He would go far-ranging to his left, behind second base, do a pirouette spin and throw. He would practice that play time after time after time, so when it came up, he would be prepared to make that play because it was part of his repertoire. Since it was already practiced, he had a comfort factor.

Also, he was able to produce with the bat. There were some times when he might have been in a slump, but everybody goes through that slump. But he never took his at-bat out onto the field with him. That was one of the amazing things about Cal. He didn't worry about what was going on with his hitting while he was out on defense.

Cal is very much a team ballplayer. He's the type of guy you want on your team and you say, "Look, the rest of you. Here is an example of what all of you could be like." I saw him early in his career, I saw him later in his career. The fact is that everything he did, he did for the team, like hitting behind runners and sacrificing himself. Yeah, there were some years when he hit .252 or .262. Why? Because he was moving runners along.

It's very taxing mentally to go out there to devote three hours a day to it. You need to have constant and vigilant attention paid. You have to be so studious for those three hours during the course of a game. Along with that, the drain of the emotional grind, the travel and everything surrounding the game itself does take its toll. It beats you up physically. It beats you up mentally. It beats you up emotionally. To go through that grind for 162 games is an awful lot to ask especially with the lifestyle. Granted, a player's lifestyle is a little easier because he will have a home base for 81 of those games, unlike an umpire who does not have home base. Therefore, an umpire is asked to start traveling in April and, conceivably, doesn't get off the road until the All-Star break for two-and-a-half days, then he's right back at it again until October.

After a few years Cal was constantly being asked, "Why don't you sit out one day?" If you played for about four, five or six years in a row, then 12 years in a row, you think one day is really going to help you? If you sat out to take that mental break and feel refreshed? To get away from everything you've done for the past 12 years? Do you think that one day is going to be like a four-week vacation? I don't think so. It really didn't necessitate Cal taking a day off. He might have had to take a couple of weeks off in order to feel refreshed or to make it seem like, "All right, I haven't done this in a long period of time."

Everybody knows the numbers - DiMaggio's 56-game hitting streak, Babe Ruth's 60 home runs, before Roger Maris hit 61, the last person to hit .400, Ted Williams - but to watch somebody accomplish those numbers and to see how they do it are different. I've seen some guys steal bases to try to get a record when they didn't need it. In that situation, they were up, 5-2, or down, 10-1, so that base is not an important base to steal at that point in time. There's not a lot of attention given to holding him on base, so he steals a base and the opposition says, "Big deal." Then you see the importance of some of these other streaks and how it adds to the winning atmosphere by adding win after win to a team's total.

The amazing thing is that Cal took a day off; Lou Gehrig sat out because he was ill. Cal sat out for other reasons. There is no telling what that number could have been had Lou Gehrig not been ill, how far it would have gone then. It would have been amazing.

Byron Nelson's Record For Consecutive PGA Tour Victories

The Pupil's View
Tom Watson

Just as Cal Ripken, Jr.'s name became synony-
mous with The Streak for his iron man efforts,
Byron Nelson is known just as well for the streak
he assembled in 1945 with 11 consecutive wins on the
PGA Tour. Nelson holds a special place in the heart of
Tom Watson as a mentor and a friend. Among
Watson's PGA Tour victories are three wins in a row at
the Byron Nelson Classic (1978-79-80). From 1981
through '98, no PGA Tour player since had won a single event three consecutive years. Watson also won the
Nelson in 1975, his second PGA Tour win. His first
came in '74 at the Western Open two weeks after the
U.S. Open where Watson first met Nelson.

11

I was playing in the U.S. Open at Winged Foot in 1974. I had the last round lead, but I shot a 79 to lose to Hale Irwin. After the round was over, I was in the locker room and in walks Byron Nelson. Before he walked in, the locker room was loud. People were leaving and people were sitting there commiserating. John Mahaffey and I were commiserating and, as soon as Byron walked in, the room went silent out of respect for the man. That's the type of respect he commands from people that play golf and outside of golf.

That was the first time I really had any direct conversation with Byron for any length of time. He said he liked the way I conducted myself and he liked my golf swing. He said if I'd like to work with him on my golf swing, he'd be happy to help out. That was the start of our long relationship both as a teacher and friend.

My father always considered Byron to be one of the best players in the game. My father is quite a historian of the game and he talked about Byron in lofty terms, considering how critical my father was about how good a player was or wasn't. He always recognized Byron along with (Ben) Hogan and (Sam) Snead as the three greatest players in the game. Bobby Jones was right in there as well. He talked about Byron always in terms of his 11 victories in a row. He said, "Well, it was in 1945 and a number of the players were still in the service." But there were still a number of players that had a chance to play against him during that year - the great players. Eleven victories in a row. Dad always said that it didn't matter whether he was playing against the best or not, it was a record that would never be broken. And I agree with that.

Winning was always something I wanted to do. That's what I strove for. When I put Byron's record in perspective with winning on the (PGA) Tour-once I got out on the Tour myself-it was just so very apparent to me that it was a record that will never be broken.

If you look at Byron's record of those 11 in a row, there were quite a few weeks in between. It wasn't just 11 weeks in a row. (After Nelson's fifth win in a row in Atlanta in early April, the next PGA Tour stop didn't occur until the Montreal Open in June). He said that when he played in the 12th tournament, after 11 wins in a row, it was a relief that he didn't win because of all the notoriety and all the pressure he was under to continue the streak.

I think Byron strove to be a great player early on in life. When he was a youngster, he and Ben Hogan played in the caddy championships in Fort Worth at the club they both caddied. Byron has always been very competitive. He loved to win and second place was a disappointment to him. He liked to get in front of people to perform. He enjoyed playing great golf, as we all do, but he enjoyed showing off his talents in front of people. When I had him in the Children's Mercy Golf Classic (in 1986, as part of an annual children's hospital charity event in which Watson hosts), he was a ham. He really loved the limelight and the opportunity to play shots in front of people. He played a number of very, very good golf shots.

He played in a handful of tournaments the following year and won a couple of them (actually six), but he wanted to retire and go into ranching. He said enough was enough-he was 34 years old.

He played in a great era of golf when he, Ben Hogan and Sam Snead competed against each other. I see that same thing happening now with Tiger Woods, David Duval and the rest of the young players. I think they're elevating themselves to play even greater golf than there would have been if there really wasn't a competition to see who was the best.

Byron has always said the amount of media attention, and the amount of time that is not yours, is eaten up by responsibilities to the media and the fans. I asked Byron, "How many autographs did you sign on a daily basis when you were in your streak?" He said, "Tom, I didn't give more than three or four autographs a day." Now everybody is there wanting your autograph for a variety of reasons.

I don't think anybody managed Byron in those days as far as helping him out with the rudimentary things you must do to operate your business or career. Today, everybody has somebody to help them out. They need their time to practice and stay proficient at the game of golf. It's a necessity, I think. There is no question about it.

The Sidekick's View

Harold "Jug" McSpaden

A *long with Byron Nelson, Harold "Jug"*
McSpaden was the other half of the tandem
known as the "Gold Dust Twins" on the PGA
Tour during the World War II years. While Nelson was
in the midst of his record-setting year with 11 consec-
utive wins in '45, McSpaden set a PGA Tour record that
same year. The most runner-up finishes (13) in one
year! McSpaden, before his death in 1996, sat down to
share his perspective of golf's most sacred record begin-
ning with when he teamed with Nelson to win the
Miami Four-Ball tournament. That tournament win
was the start of The Streak in golf.

11

We were playing exceptionally well. On that particular golf course, I was driving the ball very long and I was hitting what we used to call a "slider." Instead of hitting a hook, I'd hit a ball that would slide to the right like a slice, but it wasn't a slice. It would run after it hit like a hook would run, to the left and the course had a lot of dog leg holes to the right. Nelson and I shot a 60, 30 on each nine and that was beating most of the good players. We were competing against some great players—(Horton) Smith and (Paul) Runyon, (Walter) Hagen and (Gene) Sarazen, (Henri) Picard, (Johnny) Revolta and Craig Wood.

I hate to tell you this, but I don't think they play as well today as they did then. I think the difference is the equipment and the greens are gorgeous. I mean, they get on greens now that are really good. They're like billiard tables they're so perfect. If it looks like there's a little break, you just play for it. The pros are making eight, ten to 12-footers like there's nothing to it. For instance, in Florida–particularly where they had nothing but Bermuda (grass)–we used to putt and the ball would be bouncing all over the place. That grass was wiry.

Today, they have graphite shafts. We had steel – heavy, with thick steel shafts.

In those days, the highest compression golf ball they had was 82 compression and the best golf balls were made by Spaulding, Titleist - the company just got into the game - and Dunlop. Today, there is hardly any golf ball under 80 compression let alone 82. Today, you could have them at 90 compression, 100 compression.

The hot shots, the boys that could really hit it hard, play with 110. In other words, if you could hit it hard enough and compress it, the ball would go that much farther. That's the reason you see some of these long drivers today.

There is also a difference in technique, but marked by the difference in the clubs. Today, the pros can get different kinds of shafts, different lengths of shafts, but there wasn't near the technique back then that there is today. In fact, I was one of the first people to take pictures that were about eight or ten times slower than slow motion, which was unheard of until that point.

Today, you see all kinds of pictures like that that show you what happens. In those days, I was the first one to ever see it. I was lucky because I was in Boston when they had a camera that would take pictures that fast. In fact, I took some pictures of Nelson hitting the golf ball nine times slower than slow motion. You could see what happened to the shaft and how it would bend. You also saw what happened to the ball and how it compressed. Today, there's nothing to it. Progress.

What the tour has today, I should say, to make it more level is more good players. What surprises me today is that great players don't win more tournaments - three, four or five in a row which I have done. I won three in a row. I've won five in a row. Then all of a sudden, after trudging two or three years, you start to lose that concentration.

It's awfully hard to keep practicing and practicing and practicing. Driving yourself. We used to be criticized for playing like machines. In other words, I could go out and tell you almost exactly what I was going to do with the ball. I could make it go right or left, low or high, stop or back up or jump to the right. This game could be the most crooked game in the world. It never happened in my time, thank God, and I hope it never will.

I don't think it's possible (to ever come close to

what Nelson accomplished).

He was lucky and he played great. But there were at least two or three tournaments I could think of that he should never have won. I threw them away.

One instance, in New Orleans sticks out in my mind very much. I'm coming down to the 71st hole. I'm leading by at least one stroke or more. There are canals all over this place. I stand up on a fairway that was wide open on the right, nothing there at all. Down on the left side, there was a canal. I stood up there and hooked one right into the canal. Having been playing real well, I couldn't believe it. So I stood up and did it again. That was stupid. Then we came to the next hole, which was a par five, the 72nd hole and made a birdie four to get it tied. I shot a 67 in the playoff round. He shot a 65, played great and he deserved to win, but he never should have had the chance. I just played stupid.

I've done that two or three times in my life when there was no reason for it. No excuse, I wasn't thinking. You could almost say I was careless, but I was hitting it so well and so straight. You would have never thought I'd hit one crooked. There was no such thing as hitting it crooked. But it happens.

That year I had very bad hay fever. Nelson was staying at my home when we played the tournament in Philadelphia. We played at a golf course called the Llanerch Country Club. Pretty nice golf course and in the meantime, I was sneezing my head off. I remember going out in 40 after the first nine holes. It wouldn't have taken very much for me to pick it up and quit because I hadn't shot a 40 in nine holes in a long, long time. Anyhow, I shot a 33 on the second nine, then I had seven 33's in a row. But Byron started off with a 67 and he was leading me by seven or eight shots. It came down to the last round when he shot a 63, I believe, and I shot a 66. He beat me. I tried to chip it in on the last hole, but he would have beaten me by two strokes. We played some great golf on that golf course.

That one year, he was the only player in the history of the game that has ever averaged under 69. Average! In that particular year, my average was 69.37 for about 140 rounds. That's a lot of golf tournaments. We were driving from town to town, most of it by car. There was no such thing as going on an airplane in those days. We were playing 40 or 42 weeks a year in different towns from 250 to 500 miles away.

We were good friends. The thing about Nelson, he was the quiet type. I guess I was somewhat quiet, too. We were different, but never had a quarrel in the 15 years I played with him.

We played a lot of great golf courses and a lot of great rounds. We were playing so well that we played a lot of exhibitions. We could go onto a golf course and maybe have lunch with a committee and they'd say, "What do you think you could shoot?" I'd say, "Well, let's see the scorecard." I'd look at the scorecard and ask them, "The first question is: Is the scorecard honest?" Then I'd tell them what I thought we'd shoot. And we would do it, normally. We'd shoot a 63, 64 or 65 on the golf course.

(Byron Nelson) was the best two-wood player I ever saw, the best fairway wood player, but he wasn't the greatest chipper and putter. He was a great iron player, and we were about equal. He was a better driver than I was and I was a better chipper and putter than he was. At the same time, we teamed very well together because he rarely made a bogey. While I might make one once in awhile, I made a lot of birdies. I have made as many as seven birdies in a row. If you get something like that going, like in the Four-Ball tournament in Miami, we practically just killed the other players. We made so many birdies and eagles you wouldn't believe.

10

116

The 1906
Chicago
Cubs'
All-Time
Single
Season
Victories

The Reporter's View

Dick Schaap

Dick Schaap has authored several books, including one on the New York Yankees. So, he had to blow off the dust from the record books that covered the dynasty of the Chicago Cubs in the early part of the twentieth century. Yes, the team that is better known as the lovable losers in the last quarter of this century, set the major league record with 116 wins in 1906. Schaap, the host of ESPN's Sports Reporters and The Sporting Life with Dick Schaap on ESPN Radio, dug up some thought-provoking numbers from that era and presented some legitimate arguments on a team that was perhaps the greatest of all time, if for just one season.

The number does come trippingly off the tongue. One hundred and sixteen. It doesn't have the easy double-digit familiarity of DiMaggio's 56 or of McGwire's 70. Nor does it have the weight of Rose's 4,256 or Ryan's 5,714. But it is a baseball record that has endured longer than DiMaggio's or McGwire's, Rose's or Ryan's. It is the number of victories achieved by the Chicago Cubs during the 1906 National League season, a number that has never been matched in the National or American League, even though since then, the number of teams playing and the number of games played have expanded significantly.

This was a terrific team, the '06 Cubs, so terrific that they finished fully 20 games ahead of the second-place team, the New York Giants, even though the Giants had a Hall of Fame manager in John McGraw and a pair of Hall of Fame pitchers in Christy Mathewson and Joe McGinnity, who between them won 49 games.

The Cubs played 152 games in 1906 and lost only 36 of them for a winning percentage of .763, the best winning percentage in big-league baseball since the 1885 Chicago White Stockings, then in the National League, won 87 of their 112 games, a nifty mark of .777.

The '06 Cubs were managed by Frank Chance, who also played first base and joined with shortstop Joe Tinker and second baseman Johnny Evers, all three of them Hall of Famers, to form the double play combination celebrated in Franklin P. Adams' poem,

"Baseball's Sad Lexicon," which lamented:

"Ruthlessly pricking our gonfalon bubble,
Making a Giant hit into a double,
Words that are weighty with nothing but trouble:
Tinker to Evers to Chance."

The ace of the Chicago pitching staff was another Hall of Famer, Mordecai Peter Centennial Brown, listed in "The Baseball Encyclopedia" as "T. Brown," the T standing, of course, for "Three Finger." Old Mordecai Brown had the name Centennial because he was born in 1876 and the name "Three Finger" because, as a child, he stuck his right hand into a corn chopper, which cost him almost all of his index finger and part of two others. Three Finger Brown won 26 games and lost six for the '06 Cubs. His highest earned run average was an incredible 1.04, the second lowest in modern baseball history. (The lowest was Dutch Leonard's 1.01 eight years later.) Among Brown's teammates, Jack Pfiester went 20-8, with a 1.56 ERA, and Ed Reulbach went 19-4.

The Cubs were hardly a one-year wonder. They won the pennant again in 1907, with Tinker, Evers and Chance still turning double plays, Brown winning 20, Pfiester lowering his ERA to 1.15 and Reulbach going 17-4. With 107 victories, they finished 16 games ahead of Honus Wagner's Pittsburgh Pirates. They three-peated in 1908, with Three Finger Brown posting 29 of the team's 99 victories, slipped to second in 1909 despite 104 victories, then rebounded in 1910 when 104 victories earned them their fourth pennant in five years. In those five years, the Cubs won a total of 530 games, an average of 106 a year, an unparalleled pace. In fact, from 1904 to 1912, the Cubs won more than 90 games for nine straight seasons, a streak unequaled in National League history.

Yet as great as the Chicago Cubs were in the first decade of the twentieth century, their historic '06 season was scarred, deeply, by the fact that they lost the World Series, four games to two, to their cross-town rivals, the Chicago White Sox, an edition known as The Hitless Wonders. During the regular season, the White Sox had a team batting average of .230, the lowest in the American League, and did not have a single .280 hitter in the lineup. No one on the team hit more than two home runs. The whole team produced only seven.

In the World Series, neither the Cubs nor the White Sox were able to bat even .200, and neither hit even one home run. Including the post-season, the '06 Cubs ended up with 118 wins and 40 defeats. Three years later, the Pittsburgh Pirates won 110 during the regular season and, more important, won four and the championship in the World Series. Their overall record was 114-45. In 1927, the New York Yankees of Babe Ruth and Lou Gehrig became the first American League team to win 110 games, then swept Pittsburgh in the World Series to complete a 114-44 year. In 1954, the Cleveland Indians bettered the Yankees' regular season mark, finishing 111-43, but their record, like the '06 Cubs', was tainted by defeat in the World Series, an embarrassing defeat with four straight losses to the New York Giants.

So the 1906 Cubs' record - 116 victories in the regular season, 118 in the calendar year - remains untouched, until 1998. Then the New York Yankees managed by Joe Torre won 114 games in the regular season, an American League record, added three in the American League Division Series, four in the American League Championship Series and four in the World Series - a total of 125 victories, a big-league mark. But the Yankees lost 48 games in the regular season and two in the post-season (both in the ALCS), giving them for the year a record of 125-50, a winning percentage of .714. They broke the Cubs' record for the most victories in a calendar year, but they did not come close to eclipsing the Cubs' winning percentage.

Does this mean that "116" is the centerpiece of

the best season ever enjoyed by a major league team? My suspicion is that it does not, that you cannot divorce the regular season from the post-season, that you cannot ignore the fact that the '06 Chicago Cubs did not complete their assignment, did not win the championship of the world.

On the other hand, I am not convinced the "125," the '98 Yankees' record number, is the centerpiece, either, of the best season ever enjoyed by a major league team. I don't think you can ignore the fact that the Yankees' winning percentage, even for the full year, was lower than the 1906 Cubs', lower than the 1909 Pittsburgh Pirates' and lower than the 1927 New York Yankees'.

As much as I appreciate what the Yankees did in '98, as much as I admire the wisdom and calm of their manager, the balance and strength of their lineup, and the fact that they went through three different levels of playoffs, I still feel that the best season any baseball team ever achieved was the 1927 season of the Yankees.

It is not an easy nor an automatic decision. The '27 Yankees, in an 8-team league, finished first by 19 games. The '98 Yankees, in a 14-team league, finished first by 22 games. The '27 Yankees won four straight in the World Series by an average margin of 3.25 runs. The '98 Yankees won four straight in the World Series by the exact same average margin of 3.25 runs. On numbers alone, you could make a strong case for the latter day Yankees.

But the '27 Yankees finished 19 games ahead of a Philadelphia Athletics team that had Lefty Grove on its pitching staff and Al Simmons, Ty Cobb, Jimmie Foxx and Eddie Collins - all Hall of Famers - in its lineup. The '98 Yankees finished 22 games ahead of a Boston Red Sox team that had Pedro Martinez, Mo Vaughn and Nomar Garciaparra, a sturdy trio, but no Grove, Simmons, Cobb, Foxx and Collins. On the '27 Yankees, Babe Ruth hit 60 home runs, Lou Gehrig drove in 175 runs and Earle Combs hit .356 with 231 hits - awesome numbers. On the '98 Yankees, no one hit 30 home runs, no one drove in 125 runs and no one batted .340. On those numbers, the early-day Yankees have the stronger case.

I know the '98 Yankees are essentially better athletes than the '27 Yankees were.

I know that they're bigger and more muscular, better fed and better conditioned. I know that they have to play baseball under artificial light and on top of artificial turf, I know that they must face middle-inning specialists and late-inning specialists, an endless array of reporters including the men and women of television, a medium the earlier Yankees had never heard of.

Still, as a team for its time, my vote goes to the '27 Yankees, even as I am envious of Yankee fans for embracing history that embraces two such magnificent teams, teams that between them have cast a huge shadow over the fading magic number "116."

The Front Office View
Al Rosen

Al Rosen experienced success on the playing field and in the front office during his major league baseball career. During his playing days, Rosen was part of the 1954 Cleveland Indians who won 111 games to set an American League record. The record stood until the New York Yankees surpassed it with 114 wins in 1998. Rosen's track record in the front office included a World Series triumph with the Yankees in 1978 and a World Series appearance by the San Francisco Giants in 1989. Though Rosen played for a record-setting team in '54, he knew little about the major league record held by the 1906 Chicago Cubs until 116 popped up in '98 when the Yankees challenged that Cubs victory total.

116

I had a lot of calls from media types who wanted to know my response to the Yankees since the Indians in 1954 won 111 games, which was considered the modern record. Having worked as president of the Yankees in 1978 when we won a world championship, I have always remained a good friend of George Steinbrenner. I know Joe Torre and a lot of the coaches, so obviously it was a very exciting time for me. I must admit I had mixed emotions about them beating our American League record. Other than that, it was great for baseball and Yankee rooters.

In 1954, there wasn't the kind of media attention paid to those kinds of records as there has been in recent years. Frankly, I didn't know about the Cubs record until recently. I really thought that we held the record for the most wins by any team.

There is no one around I know who ever saw Tinker, Evers and Chance. That was their era - I saw great players in my era. I'm seeing great players now and I'm sure that 20 years from now when people talk about the great players of the past, they won't begin to think about (Lou) Boudreau, Bobby Doerr and Joe Gordon. Those players will be part of history, but they won't linger in anyone's memories because no one will have seen them play.

The post-World War II era to the mid-60s was a great era for baseball in this country. People will always remember DiMaggio, Williams, Musial, Mays and all the other greats who played in that era.

I think the '98 Yankees did exactly what I always was a proponent of - building strength through a farm system. That farm system is supplemented with players who are the type of free agents people could make deals for. You also use a lot of your young players to acquire top quality players, to go along with those who come out of your system to make up the nucleus of your club.

The guidelines were about the same in 1954. In those days, there were far more minor league teams because there were only 16 major league teams. Every club had either ownership or working agreements with one to three Triple A clubs, Double A clubs and in the B,C and D leagues. They developed their own talent, then used that talent because they were very free to trade in those days.

Everyone was subjected to being traded because they had other players in the minor leagues who could come up and take their place. Players today have guaranteed contracts. Their contracts also have no-trade or limited-trade provisions. It didn't matter in 1954.

That's the way they were built in those days because there was no such thing as free agency.

Hitting and pitching made the Indians successful in '54 and few people realize we were so deep in our pitching staff after the first four starters. We had two tremendous stoppers at the time, Don Mossi and Ray Narleski. We also had a fabulous bench. Our shortstop went down with an injury and a utility-type player named Sam Dente became the shortstop and did a remarkable job. We were so deep that (Manager Al) Lopez had the ability and foresight to move people in and out of the lineup.

We were never out of games, our pitching kept us in them. Bobby Avila led the league in hitting that year and Larry Doby led the league in home runs. Both Doby and I knocked in over 100 runs. It was a very solid ballclub.

If you want to use the word "opportunistic" very freely, it was true of our club because we had people come off the bench and deliver big pinch-hits. I still remember one game when we were behind in Boston. Hank Majeski came off the bench in the top of the ninth to hit a home run with the bases loaded. We won the game, 9-8. It was a club that took advantage of other club's weaknesses.

I have the dubious distinction of being a player whose team lost four straight in the World Series and being a president/general manager whose team had lost four straight. I know the pain and anguish of that, but I also remember the good feelings when the Yankees won in '78 and the Indians won in '48.

After we were swept in the World Series in '54, we put that behind us and we were sure we were going to win the next year, but we didn't.

In 1989, in the very famous earthquake series between Oakland and San Francisco, the Giants were swept. That should have been a fantastic series, but was marred by the earthquake. Because of the terrible damage it did to some of the infrastructure in Oakland and San Francisco and because of people losing their lives, nobody had quite the enthusiasm like they did prior to the earthquake.

You can imagine the rivalry between Oakland and San Francisco in a Bay Series.

At 5:07 on that fateful evening, the earthquake occurred, but that wasn't the reason we lost four straight. Everything pales when a tragedy like that hits.

I spent a number of years in Houston as general manager, then went to the Giants from there. My philosophy was always to build a strong infrastructure. My anchors were the scouts and the minor league instructors.

Like the '98 Yankees, we were dedicated to developing our own talent. We wanted to develop enough talent to utilize for acquiring more established players. That's what I did all the way through my career in the front office. I don't fall into that category of those who believe the Yankees' year was tarnished because it was an expansion year. I think their accomplishment is fantastic. The game is played as it is today. The schedule is what it is, the number of teams are what they are and the Yankees competed in the same framework as all the other teams and they won 125 games (including post-season wins). I don't think you can find fault in that.

I'm sure someday someone will beat that record. I think all records will be broken in every sport. It's a matter of time. Maybe someday baseball will go to a schedule with more games and with more teams.

Time revered records fall. The home run record fell and I'm a proponent of that. I think that's what the fans want. The fans are spending a lot of money to get those kinds of thrills.

I loved every minute of the '98 baseball season. I followed McGwire and Sosa and I thought it was a magnificent two-man display of sheer determination, courage and great sportsmanship. Along with the Yankees winning, I thought baseball needed a jump start and certainly it got it.

190

Hack Wilson's Single Season RBI Record

The Modern View
Tommy Davis

In 1962, Tommy Davis of the Los Angeles Dodgers drove in 153 runs, the most in the National League since Ducky Medwick drove in 154 for the St. Louis Cardinals in 1937. Only Davis, Andres Galarraga (150 in 1996) and Sammy Sosa (158 in 1998) reached the 150-RBI plateau in the National League since Medwick's total in '37. In 1930, Hack Wilson of the Chicago Cubs set the major league record with 190 RBI's in 154 games. The closest challenger was Lou Gehrig of the New York Yankees one year later with 184 driven in. Juan Gonzalez of the Texas Rangers, after driving in 101 by the '98 All-Star break, finished with 157. Davis closely watched Sosa and Gonzalez mount their RBI totals in '98 and reflected on the Wilson record total that hasn't been seriously threatened since Gehrig in '31.

190

It's unbelievable. Hack Wilson had to be phenomenal. The guys in front of him must have had great years. Had to. When you drive in 190, you don't even go to sleep, you stay at the ballpark all day. I was just hoping I could get one a game to reach 162. That was my goal and I just couldn't do it.

In 1962, we had a great family. The captain, Maury Wills, as you well know was the first to steal over 100 bases with 104. The gentleman hitting behind him was the key, I thought. I don't think people realize he was the key to everything. We called him "Junior." Jim Gilliam.

Jim was a great ballplayer. He played in Brooklyn and continued in Los Angeles. Batting second, he did so much to help Maury. You wouldn't believe it. He'd change his stance, he went from the middle of the plate to the back of the plate. The reason he went to the back of the plate was because, naturally, the catcher had to back up a little bit. If the catcher backs up, the throw is a little longer to second base. That was Jim Gilliam, he was always thinking. He took two strikes a lot, but still made contact. He hit .270 that year, then you had Willie Davis hitting third. Willie hit about .280 (.285). Between them, we had a lot of speed in the first three spots.

The scenario was this - Maury would get on by a walk, or maybe he got hit a single. There were several times we were leading 1-0, I think twice against Bob Gibson, and we had no hits. Had no hits! Maury would get on, then steal second. Gilliam would get him over to third with a ground ball to the right side. Willie

Davis would hit a ground ball because the infielders couldn't play in early in the game because of our speed on the bases. Maury would score and we'd have no hits for about five, six or seven innings. Still, we'd be winning 1-0 because of the fact that we had some great pitching in (Sandy) Koufax, (Don) Drysdale, (Johnny) Podres and (Ron) Perranoski in the bullpen.

I was hitting fourth and the gentleman behind me stood six-feet-seven, weighed about 260 and nobody wanted to pitch to him. That was big Frank Howard. Then you had Ron Fairly, John Roseboro and whomever played third. Everybody played third for us in those days. It was a combination that factored in a lot of speed and a lot of power hitting behind me. They didn't want to pitch to Frank, so they gave me a lot of pitches to hit and I took advantage of it. Besides, I could hit.

That particular year, I did get 230 hits and if you take away my 27 home runs, I still had 203 hits. I made contact quite a bit and that helped me get into that 153-RBI bracket.

With anybody who is knocking in a lot of runs, the guys in front of him must have a good year. Or at least get on base quite a bit. If you have someone with a lot of speed, who steals a lot of bases and plays the game properly, you could get a lot of runs knocked in. Frank Howard knocked in 119 runs that year batting behind me and he hit 31 home runs. Maury scored 130 runs. I scored 120 batting fourth because of Frank.

I was at 90 (RBIs) at the All-Star break. Juan Gonzalez was at 101. He's unbelievable, he just drives in those runs. Tommy Goodwin could fly. He hit first and scored a lot of runs - that's what you need.

For Sosa, I was paying attention to the RBI count. I knew he was going to hit a lot of home runs. They were giving him good pitches to hit as they were with Mark McGwire. McGwire is absolutely right when he says the second half is always tougher. That's just the way it is because everybody thinks if they didn't have a good first half, they have to work real hard to stay on the team. Some pitchers are late bloomers, who like the second half. They're tougher in the second half. The manager's going to manage different if he's in contention. They don't care who you are.

I was visualizing Drysdale, Gibson and Marichal pitching to these guys. The hitters today might get hits against them, but, I'm telling you, they would have had a hard time. In those days, you could brush a guy back, then go outside and brush a guy back again. In this day and age, I think, if you brush a guy back once, you get a warning and you can't brush him back again, or you're out of the game. I wish I could hit in this day and age. I would be very happy. I'd get on the top of the plate and make them pitch, knowing he couldn't brush me back the rest of the game.

I mean, that was the way of pitching. If you had a strike on you, the next pitch would be close and if they had another strike on you, the next pitch would be close. They wouldn't try to get you out on the third or fourth pitch, they would set you up for the fifth or sixth pitch. Then again, it might be a strike inside, so it kept you off-balanced. It made you feel like a rocking chair because that's the way they pitched. In and out, in and out. Up and down. In and out. It was tough in those days. You had to get in the batter's box and say, "Well, I don't care a bit what you're going to do the next pitch. You're just going to have to hit me."

If you brush a kid back who didn't like to be brushed back, on the next pitch, his foot would start to go toward the dugout, not toward the pitch. Sosa has hit some pitches over the plate very easily to right field because you couldn't brush him back too much.

Jim Maloney, Larry Jackson, Don Cardwell. Those were other guys who didn't care if they hit you. They were guys I felt very uncomfortable with. But I was the type of guy who waited, who didn't try to hit home runs. Just hit it hard, so I waited until the last second. I didn't go out there and try to hit the ball over the fence all the time. If I got lucky and hit a home run? Good!

Yes, it's good to hit home runs, but Sosa and Gonzalez have to hit for a high average. If they get a lot of hits, they'll do some damage.

My thing was getting the guys in. In fact, I was tougher with men on base than I was with no men on base. I didn't concentrate as much as I did with men on base. I only had 153 home runs and a little over 2,000 (2,121) hits. But I had a little over 1,000 (1,052) ribbies. So, on every two hits, on an average I was knocking in a run. I felt like the guys on base were money. They were dollar signs on the basepaths, so I needed to knock them in.

I thought Sosa did a helluva job. I was happy he was voted MVP because when your team goes to the playoffs, you've done something. With the home runs he was hitting, it was crunch time. He did a lot of good things under pressure.

The Tablesetter's View
Tom Goodwin

Fleet-footed outfielder Tom Goodwin scored 102 runs for the Texas Rangers in 1998. One of the main reasons he was hardly ever left stranded on the bases was because Juan Gonzalez and Ivan Rodriguez were hitting behind him. By the All-Star break in '98, Gonzalez drove in 101 runs and all the talk was focused on whether or not he could keep up that pace to break Hack Wilson's record of 190 in 1930. Gonzalez fell short, but not without a valiant effort. Goodwin set the table for the thumpers in a similar style to Maury Wills, who broke the one-season stolen base record with 104 in 1962 and scored 130 runs for the Los Angeles Dodgers that year with Tommy Davis and Frank Howard hitting a few notches behind him in the lineup. It should be noted that Goodwin, who wore number 42 during a portion of the time he was with the Kansas City Royals in honor of former Dodger Jackie Robinson breaking the major league color barrier, took a moment to collect himself from sharing his perspective on Gonzalez and the RBI record upon learning of the death of Joe DiMaggio on March 8, 1999. Consider Goodwin among those who follow the history of the game.

190

Obviously, Jackie Robinson was a pioneer. That's where the history begins for the non-white athletes in the major leagues. It really put all of us in a position - and I'm talking about all athletes, not just the non-whites - to where it helped the game in all aspects. Everybody knew that it was going to be one of those situations when they had to bring their best because there were going to be new ballplayers coming to town. I think Jackie really started it off and it's been up to us. Guys like Hank Aaron, Willie Mays, Dave Winfield and Reggie Jackson kept it going to where it is today. I think it's a pretty good situation.

When I was drafted by the Dodgers in '89, it really sped up my history lessons because when you come up through the organization you saw pictures of Jackie Robinson, Sandy Koufax, Roy Campanella and Don Drysdale. I was very fortunate because I didn't have to go searching for history, history came to me.

I remember (former teammate) Dave Henderson telling me when I got to Kansas City in '94, "Keep the tradition going." I really didn't know what he was talking about at the time, but he told me he wore 42 because Jackie Robinson wore 42 and it was a respectful way of saying thanks to him for what he had done. At the time I was wearing number 47 with the Royals, then I got sent down to the minors. When I came back up, 42 was available and I wanted it for that reason.

Maury Wills was very instrumental in my development. When I was in Double A, he helped me with my baserunning and my bunting. There were a lot of things he told me, like trying to hit the ball the other way, that have stuck with me to this day. He is one of those historical figures I got to know really well.

It's nice when everybody says I'm a big part of what Juan (Gonzalez) does, but honestly, you have to give credit where credit is due and that's with Juan. I know he needs people to be on base so he can do the things he does, but he still gets the big hit.

Getting on base is what I'm here to do. That's what I want to do every time I'm up to bat, but that guy who drives me in is where all the clutch work comes in.

When I'm on third and I see Juan up, I'm scared. I don't want to get too far down the line because I know what kind of liners he could hit down there. He just attacks and you can see he is one of those guys who is going to get the RBI. Juan is not going to purposely leave it up to the next guy, he wants it on his own shoulders. I think that's what separates him from the other RBI-type guys.

One hundred RBIs by the All-Star break was amazing. I never experienced anything like that before and I didn't know if I was going to have a chance to see him break the Hack Wilson record. That's what I'm talking about when I say he was going to drive in those runs. He was that way the whole first half of the season. Pitchers knew that Juan wanted to drive in those runs and they still couldn't do anything to stop him.

Juan deserves to get a lot of the credit, which I know he's getting, but that production was something awesome to see, actually. I was happy to be there to see it. Another thing special about him is that he goes about his business. He doesn't command or need any media attention. He just likes to play baseball. I was fortunate enough to be on the bases in '98 and hopefully we can do that again. It's one of those situations, though, where we can't get caught up in that talk about the Hack Wilson record. We try to play the best baseball we can day in and day out, not worrying about records that might happen. I don't think the Yankees started off '98 saying, "Okay, we're going to win 125 ballgames." I'm sure they started out saying they wanted to win the World Series and that's exactly what they did.

5,714

Nolan Ryan's All-Time Strikeout Record

The Fan's View
Ed Randall

E d Randall is considered one of the most insight-
ful and respected interviewers in sports today.
He first gained national renown and became a
fixture in local broadcast circles with his reporting on
CNN, ESPN Radio and TV Network and two New York
radio stations. With his vast experience as a play-by-
play broadcaster in the major and minor leagues and
a columnist for five teams, Randall is acknowledged
for unparalleled access to players and countless other
dignitaries in the baseball industry. He also hosts a
radio baseball show in New York called Ed Randall's
Talking Baseball. As a fan and a journalist, Randall has
an emotional perspective on the 5,714 strikeouts com-
piled by Nolan Ryan.

5,714

I get sick when I hear the name Nolan Ryan. Nothing personal, so here's a little background: I grew up in the Bronx, four miles north of Yankee Stadium. In the early 60s, the Bronx was a beautiful place to discover the world's greatest game. Despite the proximity to the stadium, all of us on the block were Mets fans. Why? Because the Johnson brothers were.

Timmy and Kenny Johnson were each packing about two bills apiece (200 pounds) by age 12. They were the toughest guys in the neighborhood. On the back fender of Timmy's bike (when bikes had fenders) was an adhesive Mets emblem. They were Mets fans. To survive, we thought it would be in our best interest to also become Mets fans. Now you understand.

The Mets of the early 60s defined futility. In their first-ever regular season game played in old Busch Stadium in St. Louis, the Cardinals scored first. On a balk! Starting pitcher Roger Craig dropped the ball going into his windup, allowing the runner from third to score.

The Mets lost more than 100 ballgames each of their first four seasons. In their third year of existence, they played a ballgame in Wrigley Field and scored 19 runs against the Cubs. Here's the joke: One guy says to another, "Did 'ya hear about the game today? The Mets scored 19 runs." The other guy answers, "Yeah, but did they win?"

In 1966, us Mets fans were giddy. There was actually a team in the world worse than ours - Leo Durocher's Chicago Cubs. (Who in their right mind could have imagined that just three years later, these same two clubs would engage in a pennant race for the ages?)

Late in the '66 season, the Mets promoted an unknown Nolan Ryan to the big club as a reward for an incredible season, just his second in pro ball. Back then, prospects received zero coverage, not like now. At Class A Greenville, he was 17-2 with a 2.51 ERA. He gave just 109 hits in 183 innings during which he struck out 272 batters. That led the league. So did his 127 walks. After he was promoted to Double A Williamsport, he was 0-2 with an 0.95 ERA. Again, amazing numbers - 19 innings, nine hits, two earned runs, 35 strikeouts and 12 walks.

He enters a game on a Sunday afternoon at Shea Stadium to face the newly-transplanted Atlanta Braves. The Mets are better than the Cubs, not the Braves. The lineup is formidable with Hank Aaron, Eddie Matthews, Rico Carty, Felipe Alou and Mack Jones. The batter is Joe Torre. Ryan tries to sneak one of his fastballs by Torre. Torre sneaks it over the fence for a home run.

The memory of that homer is indelibly etched in my mind. Why should a nondescript, meaningless home run late in the season in a meaningless ballgame be remembered a lifetime later? Because I had my first peek at Nolan Ryan. As an aspiring pitcher, he took my breath away with his raw power. That would be the first of so many other Ryan moments. Ryan would not return to the Mets until the spring of '68 when he made Manager Gil Hodges' ballclub. On Easter Sunday in Houston, he won his first major league game striking out seven of the first 10 batters he faced in a 4-0 victory. He gave just three hits in 6 2/3 innings. He eventually left the game with a blister on his finger, a problem that reappeared throughout most of his Mets career.

The Johnson brothers were gone by now from the neighborhood, moving their Future Felons of America road show elsewhere. But their impact endured. I was among the legions of young fans the late Dick Young dubbed, "The New Breed" and I loved Nolan Ryan, so much so I could imitate his windup. The Mets were as high as seventh place in the 10-team National League standings early in the season and Ryan was making his presence felt. On April 19th, he struck out the side against the Los Angeles Dodgers. No big deal. That is, until you learn he did it on nine pitches. Over his first five starts that season, covering 35 innings, he had struck out 44 batters. That included a then club-record 14 K's against the Cincinnati Reds in May. With Seaver and Koosman aboard for the fantasy trip scheduled to lift off a year later, it was Ryan who was being compared to prior fireballers (now there's a word you don't hear very often) like Bob Fuller, Sandy Koufax and Bob Gibson. But his fingers would betray him.

Here's a passage from *World Series Edition: The New York Mets Twenty-Five Years of Baseball Magic*:

> Unfortunately, as good as he was, Ryan had a problem. In almost every start he developed a blister on the middle finger of his pitching hand. Trainer Gus Mauch, a veteran of many seasons, remembered that pickle brine had a tendency to toughen skin. So one day Mauch stopped in a delicatessen near the Concourse Plaza Hotel in the Bronx where he and his wife, Mary, maintained an apartment. Mauch purchased a couple of kosher pickles and asked for some extra brine.
>
> Mauch instructed Ryan to dip his finger in the pickle brine between starts, hoping it would toughen the skin. For awhile, the brine appeared to have a positive effect. When reporters questioned Mauch about the details of the miracle brine that enabled Ryan to keep throwing sans blisters, the trainer obliged with the type of brine and the name of the delicatessen where he

had purchased it. The very next day, the Bronx delicatessen had a sign in its window - "Nolan Ryan buys his pickle brine here."

This being New York, the whole city knew about the pickle brine caper. Mention the name Nolan Ryan to any lifelong Mets fan now 30 years later and they invariably will use the words 'pickle brine' in a sentence. But the remedy was only a temporary one.

By the end of July, Ryan had developed blisters severe enough to force him onto the disabled list. But that wasn't his only problem. Army Reserve duty called as war raged on the other side of the world. Blisters and all, he went on two weeks of duty. What had started as the fulfillment of a promise ended in disappointment and frustration. Despite 133 strikeouts in 134 innings of work, Nolan Ryan never won another game during that 1968 season.

But it was during the Miracle Mets improbable run to the World Championship the following year that Ryan is remembered for one conversation and one pitch. Coming home to Shea Stadium in the first-ever National League Championship Series, the Mets held a two-games-to-none lead over Atlanta in what was then a best-of-five format.

In Game Three, Mets starter Gary Gentry had runners at second and third and was down, 2-0. When Rico Carty pulled a long drive to left that was barely foul, Manager Gil Hodges had seen enough, making a seminal move in a season of seminal moves. It was only the third inning, far too early for the closers of the day, Tug McGraw and Ron Taylor. The call went to Ryan. Having missed most of the season with injuries and military obligations, he was completely unfamiliar to Carty, the "Beeg Boy" who could turn on a fastball with the best of them.

As Ryan warmed, Carty conferred in the on-deck circle with Orlando Cepeda, acquired at the start of the season from the Cardinals for holdout catcher Joe

Torre. When Carty asked Cepeda for a scouting report, Cepeda said words to the effect, "You're not gonna believe this. He throws smoke."

Gentry had been lifted with a count of 1-and-2. Ryan went into his windup and threw a fastball that Rico Carty never saw to retire the side. Despite giving up a two-run homer to Cepeda, Ryan pitched four scoreless innings the rest of the way as the Mets rallied to complete the three-game sweep.

Years later, all I remember is that conversation.

Ryan's remaining two seasons in New York, 1970 and '71, were basically nondescript affairs. He would be overpowering with command one game, then follow it five days later with fits of wildness. That drove Gil Hodges nuts. He had convinced himself that Ryan would be consigned to the tallest of all scrapheaps for pitchers: hard throwers with unfulfilled potential.

Never once was Ryan regarded by the organization, the press or the fans in the same reverential tones reserved for Tom Seaver and Jerry Koosman. Tell a Mets fan to name pitchers and the response would always be the same refrain: Seaver and Koosman. It was never Seaver and Ryan. Despite his unbounded frustration, Ryan got along with everyone, happy to be part of such a wealth of pitching talent.

Which brings us to a dreary, December day in '71 when he was traded away. For me, it is another moment frozen in time. I was in Yankee Stadium when Chris Chambliss beat the Royals, there again the night Reggie hit the three homers on three swings against three different pitchers.

I was matriculating at Fordham University, the noted Jesuit community for higher learning. Like any other day when my classes had ended, I emigrated to the college radio station, WFUV, preparing for what would be this fantastically successful professional broadcasting career. In the back room, which served as the newsroom, the kids were preparing for that night's early evening newscast. Our only source for news was the old, black AP machine, which rested on a set of springs and rocked gently back and forth as it spilled its guts.

I almost spilled mine when I learned that as the Winter Meetings were closing in Scottsdale, Ariz., the Mets had traded Ryan, fellow pitcher Don Rose, promising outfielder Leroy Stanton, who was as highly regarded as Ryan, and catcher Francisco Estrada to the California Angels for Jim Fregosi. Four-for-one. The other way!

Whitey Herzog ran the Mets minor league department at the time. When he was told the Mets had traded Stanton, Rose and Estrada for Fregosi, he reacted with a shriek of, "What?" When he was told Ryan was in the deal, too, he raised his voice a few more levels with another, "What?"

For moi, it was devastating news. It could have been Ryan straight up for the Babe in his prime, I didn't care. Bottom line was I could no longer snap on WOR-TV and watch my boy check everyone's manhood at the door.

Without me monitoring his progress, Nolan Ryan won 295 games and struck out just 5,221 batters after leaving New York. The noted philosopher, Oscar Gamble, once said a good night against Nolan Ryan was "0-for-4 and don't get hit in the head." Reggie Jackson said hitting against Ryan was like trying to drink coffee with a fork. The late, great Jim Murray put it best: "His arm should hang in the Smithsonian - right next to the Spirit of St. Louis."

At the January press conference introducing the 1999 Hall of Fame class, I finally got to ask Ryan the question I had saved for nearly 30 years, "For years after you left New York, Nolan, there was this theory that you never would have experienced the degree of success you eventually did had you remained here. They said you were uncomfortable in the big city, that Ruth didn't like it here, there were the blisters and the military obligations interrupting your season. Did you ever hear that and do you agree with it?"

Best damn question of the press conference if you ask me.

This was part of his answer, "Let's say this, being from Texas - small-town, rural Texas - living in New York was definitely an adjustment. Each and every year I'd have been there, there would have been a larger comfort zone and I would have developed a liking for New York."

Shoot me, he just confirmed my worst fears! To assume New York would have eaten up Nolan Ryan would be to insult his greatness, intelligence and work ethic.

So how do you think it made me feel when, near the end of his career, Ryan told me in Yankee Stadium he watched my *Talking Baseball* series at home in Texas? I was so happy I didn't even think to stick out my tongue and tell him that I'm not on his all-time career strikeout list.

Thank you, Johnson brothers for "suggesting" I root for the Mets. And even though I can still imitate Nolan Ryan's windup to this day, the whole thing still makes me sick.

The Veteran's View

Bob Feller

Hall of Fame pitcher Bob Feller broke into the majors at age 18 and recorded 2,581 strikeouts in his 18-year career with the Cleveland Indians. In 1946, his first full season after missing almost four full seasons in the prime of his career serving in World War II, Feller set an American League record at the time by striking out 348 hitters. The record held up until 1973 when Nolan Ryan struck out 383. Though Feller led the A.L. in strikeouts seven different seasons, the individual numbers dear to his heart were in complete games (279 career CG's) as you'll find in his perspective of Ryan's all-time career strikeout record.

5,714

I've seen Nolan pitch from time to time. He has pitched more great games, seven no-hitters with more strikeouts than any pitcher in history, so he belongs in the Hall of Fame. He deserves to be in the first time around. Also, he has done a good job for baseball.

His winning record (324-292) isn't all that great. His biggest problem as a pitcher was holding a one-run lead in the last couple of innings during his career because he didn't pace himself. One might say some of the clubs he was with weren't too good. Well, neither was Walter Johnson or yours truly. The Cleveland Indians weren't the New York Yankees all the time either when I was with them, particularly before the war. You can't always be on a pennant winner or a world championship ballclub like some of the guys such as Whitey Ford.

Walter Johnson was a great pitcher. He pitched a lot of low-run games. More than half of his career was in the dead ball era. The last half of his career, from 1920 to '27 when he retired, was with the live ball, which came into being in 1920 when they put the rubber in the ball so Ruth could hit home runs and make people forget the Black Sox Scandal (1919). At least that was the idea and it seemed to have worked. There were some very good pitchers in those days. Johnson was a sidearm pitcher who had no curveball whatsoever. His curveball wasn't even a wrinkle. All he could do was throw hard.

Rube Waddell, I never knew. Back in 1904, he struck out 343 or 349 - the number listed in *The*

Baseball Encyclopedia - in one year. There's an argument about that. People say he was a carouser, had no self-discipline and a very short career (13 years). He couldn't stand prosperity and was somewhat of a character. I guess Connie Mack had a heckuva time keeping him disciplined, but he was a great pitcher (elected to the Hall of Fame in 1946 with 2,316 strikeouts officially).

Lefty Grove had a lot of great strikeout years (American League strikeout leader from 1925-'31). He threw as hard as anybody, I understand. He was all washed up when I saw him - I never saw him in his prime. In fact, when I pitched against him, he couldn't even break a glass, but he still had good control and he was a winning pitcher for the Red Sox (15-4 in 1939 with 81 strikeouts at age 39).

Rather than compare pitchers of 50 years ago or 100 years ago, you have to compare them to their contemporaries. It goes for all men, like George Washington and Gen. Patton. Who was the greatest person in what walk of life like politics, art or whatever? That's very difficult to choose and it's very, very arguable. Everybody has their own hero, everybody thinks that somebody is better than another person. That's all right, that's what this world is all about. You have to make up your own mind.

Today, conditions are much different than they were in my time when I hit my prime just before World War II and right after World War II. The ballparks are smaller. A lot more night ball is one of the factors. It's more difficult to hit at night than in the daytime, in my opinion, not much more, but some, particularly on the breaking ball. It's harder to hit a breaking ball at night.

Night ball came into the major leagues in 1935. Cincinnati got the first lights in 1935. I heard that game on the radio. In fact, I saw the first night game ever played, in Des Moines, Iowa, 1930. That was a minor league game. I pitched the first night game ever played in St. Louis, incidentally, in 1940. We got our lights in Cleveland in 1939. Philadelphia got their lights in 1939. They were the first ones in the American League. We were a week later than the Philadelphia Athletics. The Red Sox were very slow with their lights, and, of course, the Cubs didn't get theirs until just a few years ago.

Most of my records in strikeouts were broken in day ball. Yes, I pitched well at night, but I preferred to pitch in the daytime. Always did. All three of my no-hitters were in day ball. The air was different and the humidity was a lot lower. You wouldn't get so wet and sweaty and clammy. Of course, it might be hot, but you can always control that with changing jerseys and shirts. I never struck out more than 16 in one game at night. I struck out 17 and 18 in day ball.

It's much easier to strike out the hitters now than it was in those days because the money's in the long ball. Nobody just goes up there and puts the ball in play anymore. They're swinging from their heels because they don't pay as much money for singles, doubles or bunts. In those days, if a guy got two strikes, or even one strike, they cut back on their swing. There's no stigma or embarrassment anymore to striking out, but there used to be.

I didn't try to strike everybody out. I would ease up, try to get by and try to win the ballgame, which to me is more important than strikeouts. To have that little extra stuff to hold that one-run lead in the seventh, eighth or ninth if you're in a close ballgame. After you get by the fourth or fifth inning and you get one or two outs, whether you have a lead or not, you get hitters who don't hit you. You can get them out fairly easily when you ease up on them and try to make them hit the ball. To get them out on one or two pitches, you don't really bear down on them where they'll foul off a few, then you throw a ball or two and wind up throwing six or seven pitches to them. You want to get rid of them in a hurry and you can save several pitches that way in the heart of the ballgame. You can save your good stuff for the last couple of innings, or for the tough guys who do hit you in the heart of the batting order, the ones you have to bear down on. That's what I used to do and that's why I pitched so many complete games.

Usually, it was a good gamble, but you knew that from your own experience. You have it filed in the little book in your head. You know these hitters because there were only seven other teams you had to worry about. There were only eight teams in the league. It's not like it is now. You don't know the hitters very well, their weakness or their strong points. There are so darned many of them in interleague play. All you know are rumors or what somebody knows about them from playing with them or against them. It has made it more difficult to find the weaknesses of the hitters you're pitching against today.

You've got all these stats from computer printouts, but you don't know who was pitching against these guys. If a fella had your same style, such as the way I threw - overhand to left-handers and three-quarters fastball, curveball, slider, changeup occasionally - I'd talk to him. I wouldn't even look at the stats from a left-hander, or a sinkerball pitcher or somebody who throws knuckleballs. Like Nolan Ryan, he'd look at the ones similar to the ones I had because he pitched like I did, so he and I would get along fine. Like Allie Reynolds and I, we would discuss those things.

I never drank during my career, never used tobacco. I worked hard, did a lot of physical exercises - calisthenics and Canadian Air Force exercises. I was aboard ship for three years where I did a lot of exercises. I was out for four years in World War II. In fact, I joined the Navy two days after Pearl Harbor, went to war college, then rode the battleship Alabama for three years. I'm very proud of my military career and that I did a job which was necessary. I'm no hero. The heroes are the ones who didn't come back, in my opinion.

I retired from the Indians when I was only 37, but

I had other things I wanted to do. I wasn't doing that well. The manager we had at the time, Al Lopez, wasn't pitching me very much and it was time to get moving. Just after I retired, the manager left and went to Chicago. I have nothing against Al Lopez - he just didn't like the way I was pitching. He didn't feel I was throwing as hard as I did in my prime. I was doing it with curves and sliders, and doing it with control. I knew the hitters.

Nolan had a better than average curve. He didn't have a great curve, but he had a great fastball and his curve was so deceptive. It broke fast and sharp. (Sandy) Koufax had a real good curveball and all those other great pitchers had better curveballs than Nolan, but it was such a surprise to see his curveball paralyze the hitters. He could throw hard. He was a big guy, 6-2, a lot bigger than I am. My best playing weight was 183. I don't know what his was, but I'm sure it was over 200. He kept himself in great condition by his daily routine of stretching and stamina building exercises.

Twenty wins was a big deal in those days and still is, though not nearly as many pitchers are winning 20 as they used to. You go to the relief pitcher and he gets the save. You have the set-up guy coming in. The manager overmanages like crazy nowadays and the starting pitchers don't know how to pace themselves. They can't take a deep breath or two and tighten up their belt to pitch the eighth or ninth inning and hold that one-run lead. The managers don't give them a chance to. They take them out no matter what the situation is.

A pitcher gets a little ahead in a ballgame and he keeps looking to the bullpen for someone to pick him up after the fifth inning. I don't think any of them have much pride in pitching complete games anymore. I don't even think the manager intends to let him pitch a complete game. Why? I don't know, even if he has a ten-run lead. I mean, it's ridiculous. "Well, you have to save little for their next game." You can't save anything for the next game. You just don't save a muscle - you gotta use it. It might give him more stamina. They might need the extra two innings to build up their confidence. I used to throw 130 to 140 pitches a game, usually 125 to 135 because I allowed them to foul off the ball. Or if I was a little wild, I'd walk a few and get 3-and-2 on everybody. You might get tired. You didn't think you were, but you might lose a little of your stuff. Usually, you knew that yourself as well as anybody else.

I pitched 36 complete games after my first year out of the Navy. I hadn't pitched in four years and pitched 36 complete games in 1946, which were the most complete games since 1916 and to this very day. That was the best year since four years before the live ball. (Grover) Alexander pitched 38 complete games in 1916 and Johnson pitched 36 in 1916.

Conclusion

From reading the preceding perspectives one might conclude that for any athlete, in this modern age, to seriously challenge any of these sacred records, they would need to have the ability to cope with the media attention that would surely ensue. As you have probably figured out, any individual positioning for a record-breaking performance will need to be poised, not only on the field of play, but willing to endure the pressure of the scrutiny.

That's what differentiated the accomplishment of Mark McGwire in 1998 from the Super Bowl champion Denver Broncos that same season. As the pressure mounted in the final month of the baseball season, McGwire, with the push of Sammy Sosa in the Home Run Derby, met the challenge on the baseball field and somehow managed to keep himself together though under the microscopic attention. Although the Broncos ultimately won the big prize, the team found out what any team or individual must endure as the attention increases upon approaching a reverential milestone. Denver felt the scrutiny as the Broncos approached Miami's 17-0 record.

Does that diminish what the Broncos accomplished in '98? Or what the Yankees accomplished despite falling three short of breaking the regular season record held by the 1906 Cubs? Or what Juan Gonzalez accomplished during a Most Valuable Player season when his RBI count fell well below the Hack Wilson standard? Of course not. Each feat was and is outstanding in its own right, but it only serves to notice the greatness of the sacred records.

It could also be concluded that those who have contributed perspectives in this book have the same reverence for a few of the most distinguishable numbers in the twentieth century. Keep in mind that these are folks who have either played the game or have covered it extensively. It seems that the one constant, both in the pages of this book and in casual conversation, is that Joe DiMaggio's record 56-game hitting streak somehow enters the picture. It's easy to see why.

Rest in peace, Joe.

Greg Echlin

B ased in Kansas City, Greg Echlin is a full-time executive sports producer at a radio station and has contributed several written sports pieces to newspapers and magazines across the country. He also worked behind the scenes as the Managing Editor for the popular *Arrowhead: Home of the Chiefs*, released in 1997. As a sports reporter, Echlin has covered the top sporting events, including the Super Bowl, the World Series and the Final Four throughout his 20-plus years in the business.

01095

7 08850 11074 9